ENOUGH ABOUT YOU

Notes toward the New Autobiography

—m—

David Shields

Soft Skull Press
Brooklyn

Library of Congress Cataloging-in-Publication Data is available upon request.

ISBN-10: 1-59376-219-4
ISBN-13: 978-1-59376-219-3

Cover design by Alvaro Villanueva
Interior design by Maria Mendez, Neuwirth & Associates, Inc.
Printed in the United States of America

Soft Skull Press
An Imprint of Counterpoint LLC
2117 Fourth Street
Suite D
Berkeley, CA 94710

www.softskull.com
www.counterpointpress.com

Distributed by Publishers Group West

10 9 8 7 6 5 4 3 2 1

Praise for the hardcover edition of
Enough About You:
Notes toward a New Autobiography

"Novelist and cultural commentator Shields explores 'his own damned, doomed character' in this plum collection of vignettes. What he's trying to get at in these pages is the mystery of identity, cutting to the bone as he explores the 'impulse to write autobiographically, to turn oneself into one's subject.' Shields makes it easy to identify with his confusions and screw-ups and ambivalences, but his insightfulness and careful consideration are his canny talent. Gladdeningly inclusive, like a hug from Walt Whitman: declarative and fraught and good." —*Kirkus Reviews*

"*Enough About You* attempts to move beyond those self-created mythologies we save for first dates and talk show appearances. Shields wants to capture the lumps in our throats, the ambivalences and misconnections we don't know how to express. David Shields uses gimmicks and sidelong glances to catch the truth with its pants down. If we can hold our impatience at bay, the technique works, provoking the reader to rethink the clumps of chronological data that pass for biography, so inadequate to convey the slippery slopes of a human life." —Joy Press, *Village Voice*

"He recognizes the absurd self-absorption inherent in memoir, and that goes a long way in a book about the subject . . . a thoroughly entertaining literary memoir . . . should appeal to memoir enthusiasts looking for perceptive and humorous views on our own perpetual self-fascination." —*Amazon.com*

"*Enough About You* works because of the writer's fearless honesty . . . in *Enough About You*, Shields ditches the outside subject matter to confront his narcissism head-on, a particularly potent theme in these self-absorbed times." —J. Peder Zane, *Raleigh News & Observer*

"[I]n an era of confessional memoirs, reality television, celebrity biographies, and Web cams broadcasting the details of everyday lives . . . Shields takes up autobiography as a strategy to unravel what it means to be human in a media-saturated culture . . . a kind of mutated memoir that pokes fun at our endless navel-gazing."
—Andrew Engelson, *Seattle Post-Intelligencer*

"[A]mazing . . . intriguing . . . fun . . . breezy . . . pithy . . . lively . . . wily . . . diverting . . . insouciant . . . ." —*Booklist*

"*Enough About You* reclaims the [autobiography] genre and lifts it to soaring new heights." —Rochelle Renford, *Weekly Planet*

"Shields turns out a series of uncommon and provocative discussions about what it's like to play, to watch, to be watched, to be judged, to feel weak, to feel strong, and to not quite know what to feel." —Eric Neel, *ESPN.com*

"The very act of autobiography makes for the motor of one of the most unique, intriguing, and entertaining memoirs in recent memory. In a style that's funny and fresh, matchless and moving, he discourses on subjects literary and personal, offering sparkling anecdotes from his life and engaging ruminations on others, all borne along by a bubbling undercurrent of interest in life stories, why we tell them, and the ways we do." —*Internet Book Info*

"Shields is a pioneering writer, breaking new ground. The future of personal narrative looks a lot like this book." —Robert Clark

"In this book on confession, self-reflection, and self-absorption, David Shields gets to several essential features of contemporary American character, and he does it with wit, intelligence, and a kind of insight that is all the more impressive because of its epigrammatic eloquence. The result is sometimes funny, sometimes profound, sometimes moving, and sometimes all these things at once." —Charles Baxter

"*Enough About You* is an autobiography that complicates the process of autobiographical writing, of talking about oneself directly, at every turn. If consciousness is irrevocably fragmented, Shields is pretty good at putting the pieces back together. 'Seamless' would be the wrong word for this book, but Shields's ability to weave a coherent and rather likable voice—ironic, self-implicating, blackly funny, hopeful—through these disjointed passages is impressive." —Elaine Blair, *Newsday*

"Shields examines the impulse to write about our experiences, turning our lives into works of art. Shields pulls this off with candor and grace to such an extent that we can see ourselves shining through." —Ron Ratliff, *Library Journal*

"Shields manages a great feat with his new book, a meditation on self-reflection: he invites us into his mind as he turns his life into narrative." —*Speed Reader*

For
Laurie and Natalie

Contents

—ᗰᗰ—

I know of nothing more difficult than knowing who you are, and having the courage to share the reasons for the catastrophe of your character with the world.

—William Gass

Ross McElwee
The Knife in the Brain

Foreword to David Shields's *Enough About You:*
Notes toward the New Autobiography

IN THIS BOOK, David Shields is obsessed with what it means to
be an autobiographical writer. Autobiography is where DNA's
double helix gets bent and twisted, turns in on itself, tangles and
knots its strands, and yields its greatest challenges to the writer
and, in the case of David Shields, considerable rewards for the
reader.

Shields has written autobiographical nonfiction and autobiographical fiction. In his second novel, *Dead Languages*, which
deploys stuttering as a metaphor for the difficulty of human communication, the character based on David's father is described in
all of his flawed idiosyncrasy. When David's father read the fictional depiction of himself in *Dead Languages*, he was, according
to Shields, somewhat angry about the way his fictional counter-
part was laid bare. In a letter to his father in *Enough About You*,
Shields argues that the portrait of his father is a sympathetic one

that honors the complexity of living by striving for a kind of painful truth, rather than sentimentality. However, Shields also acknowledges that his father's response to this is probably, "Yeah, yeah, but how would *he* like it if I wrote a book in which all of *his* most embarrassing moments had been resurrected for all to see?" Point taken, but I side with the author here.

In nonfiction, there's usually no attempt to cloak identities in even the most translucent fictional guises, yet there is never anything mean or menacing about the way in which Shields writes about the people in his life. Insightful irony, perhaps, but nothing cruel. He's too much in love, albeit nervously, with life and the living.

I'm not a writer; I'm an autobiographical documentary filmmaker. I find utterly familiar Shields's struggle with maintaining sufficient distance from life (in order to write about it) while per force having to remain immersed in life in order to have anything to observe. This defines the vexing and paradoxical terrain of autobiography, no matter what the medium. Shields's work artfully weaves into a single thematic braid acute observations about, on the one hand, the world around him and, on the other, his own internal state. *Enough About You* is a crazy quilt of *seemingly* random swatches: appreciations of Bill Murray and Adam Sandler, Vince Carter and Bob Knight; explorations of stuttering, sex, vicariousness, celebrity; exegeses of Rousseau, Nabokov, Renata Adler; a dream about his father. Shields *seems* to gather his material the way a cinéma vérité filmmaker gathers random moments of unscripted reality—a shot here, a scene there—responding to what is interesting to him at the moment. I've twice italicized the word "seem," as only the most inattentive reader will find the structure of the book random. *Enough About You* is held together by its powerfully unfolding argument that the "new autobiography" is not straight-ahead memoir but pointillistic collage that uses self as theme-carrier or host: each of us, plumbed deeply enough and from enough angles, contains the entire human condition.

Autobiographical writing has a long and noble lineage. St. Augustine's *Confessions* set the form in motion nearly two thousand years ago. Nineteenth-century England saw an explosion of autobiographical essayists—Lamb, Hazlitt, Ruskin, DeQuincey. And in our own New World, Emerson observed of his contemporaries, "The key to the period seemed to be that the mind had become aware of itself. There was a new consciousness. The young men were born with knives in their brains, a tendency to introversion, self-dissection, anatomizing of motives." *Enough About You* is a book about taking the knife in your brain and twisting it into brilliant literary art. It also is an example of same.

I.

PROLOGUE

In Praise of Reality

—w—

And I shall essay to be.

—Emerson

STANDARD OPERATING PROCEDURE for fiction writers is to disavow any but the most insignificant link between the life lived and the novel written; similarly, for nonfiction writers, the main impulse is to insist upon the unassailable verisimilitude of the book they've produced. I've written three works of fiction and—counting this book—three works of nonfiction, and whenever I'm discussing the supposed reality of a work of nonfiction, I inevitably (and rapidly) move the conversation over to a contemplation of the ways in which I've fudged facts, exaggerated my emotions, cast myself as a symbolic figure, and invented freely. So, too, whenever anyone asks me about the origins of a work of fiction, I always forget to say, "I made it all up," and instead start talking about, for lack of a better term, real life.

Both of my parents were journalists. For many years my mother was the West Coast correspondent for the *Nation*. My father, now ninety, wrote for dozens of left-wing publications and organizations and for the last twenty years has been a sports reporter for a weekly newspaper in suburban San Francisco. "The true poem," my father likes to say, quoting Walt Whitman, "is the daily paper." When I was growing up, the *New York Times* was air-mailed to our house every day. Mornings, I would frequently find on the kitchen counter an article neatly scissored out of the *Times* for me to read as a model of journalistic something or other. (Actually, I may have made this detail up, but it sounds right, it feels right, maybe it happened once; I'm going to leave it in.) I was the editor of my junior high school newspaper. I was the editor of my high school newspaper. Woodward and Bernstein were my heroes. My parents' heroes, interestingly enough, weren't journalists but what they called "real writers": Thomas Wolfe, John Steinbeck, Saul Bellow.

My father stammered slightly, and in the verbal hothouse that was our family (dinner-table conversations always felt like a newsroom at deadline), I took his halting speech and turned it into a full-blown stutter. My stutter not only qualified any ambition I might have had to become a journalist—I couldn't imagine how I'd ever be able to imitate my mother's acquaintance Daniel Schorr and confidently ask a question at a presidential press conference—but also made me, in general, wary of any too direct discourse. In graduate school, when I studied deconstruction, it all seemed very self-evident. Language as self-canceling reverb that is always only communicating itself? I felt like I knew this from the inside out since I was six years old. In a stutterer's mind and mouth, everything is up for grabs.

I have a very vivid memory of being assigned to read *The Grapes of Wrath* as a junior in high school and playing hooky from my homework to read *Fear and Loathing on the Campaign Trail*. Steinbeck's humorlessness, sentimentality, and sledgehammer symbolism hardly had a chance against Hunter S. Thompson's comedy, nihilism, and free-association. I loved how easily *Fear and Loathing* mixed reportage or pseudo-reportage with glimmers of memoir. My sister and I had a rather fierce debate about the authenticity of a scene in which Thompson has a conversation with Richard Nixon at an adjoining urinal. She wrote to Thompson to ask him which of us was right. I was wrong; he called me a "pencil-necked geek" for thinking the scene had been invented.

During freshman orientation, I joined the *Brown Daily Herald*, but by February I'd quit—or perhaps I was fired—when there was a big brouhaha surrounding the fact that I'd made stuff up. I started spending long hours in the Marxist bookstore just off campus, reading and eating my lunch bought at McDonald's; I loved slurping coffee milkshakes while reading and rereading Sartre's *The Words*. I closed the library nearly every night for four years; at the end of one particularly productive work session, I actually scratched into the concrete wall above my carrel, "I shall dethrone Shakespeare." Fueled by such ambition, I was a good bet for graduate school, where my first creative writing instructor said she wished she were as famous to the world as she was to herself, and my second creative writing instructor said that if he had to do it over again, he'd have become a screenwriter.

On my breakneck tour of European capitals the summer after grad school, I carried in my backpack two books: García Márquez's *One Hundred Years of Solitude* and Proust's *Swann's Way.* Just as Steinbeck's allegory had bored me and Thompson's meditation on the real had enthralled me, García Márquez failed to hold my attention and Proust become a year-long addiction. I loved how Marcel was both sort of the author and sort of a character; how the book was both a work of fiction and a philosophical treatise; how it could talk about whatever it wanted to for as long as it wanted to; how its deepest plot was uncovering the process by which it came into being.

And yet my first novel was pretty much whole-cloth invention. My second book was an extremely autobiographical growing-up novel. My last book of fiction was a collection of stories, many of which read more like essays. My next book was a collage memoir. My most recent book was a diary of a basketball season. You can see, I hope, how I'm going in the wrong direction from how I'm supposed to be going.

And now this: not only an autobiographical book but a book about the impulse to write autobiographically, to turn oneself into one's subject. A fiction writer (an ex-fiction writer?), knowing full well how invented such representations are, is hopelessly, futilely drawn toward representations of the real. He's bored by out-and-out fabrication, by himself and others; bored by invented plots and invented characters. He wants to explore his own damn, doomed character. He wants to cut to the absolute bone. Everything else seems like so much gimmickry. This book is an attempt to embody these ideas, to make the case that the only real journey is deeper inside and the only serious subject is the mystery of identity—mine, especially, but yours, too, I promise. Here, in other words, is how I give you me. Here, also, is how I give you you. Here, finally, is how you give me me.

II.

M-M-ME

Rousseau's Distance

—⁓〰⁓—

In *THE CONFESSIONS*, Rousseau claims to be puzzled by the fact that he must wait until he stops thinking before he's able to begin writing. He wonders why his passions are quick to erupt while his thoughts are slow to form. It confuses him that perception is enhanced by temporal and psychic distance, that memory produces illuminations which observation didn't. He can't comprehend why, given time, he's able to write eloquently, whereas in conversation he's nervously inarticulate.

Rousseau, realizing that he needs to be detached in order to apprehend let alone convey meaning, suggests that he could carry on a very clever conversation through the mail. Such an arrangement establishes distance between himself and his correspondent

so that he can control the interaction, which is precisely the relationship he wants to cultivate between himself and the reader of
The Confessions. "With sufficient leisure I can compose excellent
impromptus," he claims, but the whole point of impromptus is,
of course, that they're unplanned. In truth, Rousseau despises
clever conversation.

"One might say that my heart and mind do not belong
to the same person," he writes. The reader implicitly is the
"one" of "one might say," but if I believe that Rousseau's mind
and heart are irreparably severed, I'm remaining oblivious of
the fact that Rousseau has already resolved such a division by
writing. He's writing and therefore thinking when he states,
"I feel everything and see nothing"; the sentence itself is a perception, and this distillation can occur only over time. One
of the recurrent and fundamental ironies of *The Confessions*
is that Rousseau lucidly and energetically conveys his inability to write, impeccably communicating the impossibility of
communication.

He complains that he's simply unable to "produce anything,
pen in hand, in front of my table and paper," whereas he's able
to write in his mind when walking amidst rocks and forests.
Rousseau locates his inspiration in nature, but he nevertheless
acknowledges the need for mediation between himself, on the
one hand, and his free-flowing instincts and thoughts, on the
other, if he is to be able to express himself. He's so obsessed with
the creative act that he demands distance from it in order to
convey his passion. He explains his need for detachment by saying that he's unable to "write down immediately what occurs to
me" or write "works which require to be written with a certain

lightness of style, such as letters." He succeeds better in "works which require labor." And yet what is *The Confessions* if not a letter from Rousseau to the reader written with a "certain lightness of style"?

Rousseau seems to be amazed by the conundrum that he can see clearly only what he remembers and not what he perceives, but the entire book is a dramatization of the power of memory: "Of all that is said, of all that is done, of all that goes on in my presence, I feel nothing, I see through nothing. The outward sign is the only thing that strikes me. But later, all comes back to me. Then from what people have said or done, I discover what they have thought." Only when he's separated from passion and removed from reality is Rousseau able to be alone, write, and then understand the past by imagining it.

For Rousseau, language represents the freedom to explore and then admit especially what is disturbing, memorable, and offensive. Aware that he tends to blurt out precisely what he wants to suppress, he notes that even socialites "frequently let fall awkward and ill-timed remarks." Discussing a mild (and oblique) faux pas he committed, he claims he had no desire to offend his hostess, "a woman who was too amiable not to have made herself somewhat talked about," then mocks himself by saying, "Such are the flashes of genius which escape me when I attempt to speak without having anything to say." But of course he meant to offend this too amiable woman; of course he had something to say; of course I love Rousseau because his paradoxes are precisely my paradoxes—detachment as a sort of intimacy, society as an isolation tank, language (private, written, wrought) as both prison house and paradise.

Two Houses of Language

—⟋⟍—

I REMEMBER ARRIVING in Iowa City, standing in the middle of downtown, and asking someone, "Where's downtown Iowa City?" I remember meeting the administrator of the Writers' Workshop, experiencing the feeling that she was somehow my long lost older sister, and never coming remotely close to losing that feeling. I remember hearing my highly alliterative short story, "The Gorgeous Green of the Hedges," gently demolished in my first workshop and, upon returning to my apartment, eating bowl after bowl of mint-chip ice cream until the room spun. I remember admiring how some of my classmates had figured out how to get their own personality onto the page. At the time, I wrote like Thomas Hardy and I thought, regarding my classmates and their ability to convert their speaking voice into a narrative voice, "I can do that . . . or if not, I better learn." I remember one of my classmates seeing me at a Northrop Frye lecture and saying, as a sort of accusation, "I thought I'd see you here." (My work was heavy on the symbolism.) I remember thinking nothing of knocking on a friend's door at eleven o'clock at night to get his reaction to a new story I'd written; he didn't like it, so he praised, at ludicrous length, my delicate application of Liquid Paper. I remember becoming an instantaneously and excessively devoted fan of the Iowa men's basketball team; my first novel came out of that. I remember being a patient in the University of Iowa Speech and Hearing Clinic and being overwhelmed by the paradox that as a writer I was learning to manipulate words but that as a stutterer I was at the mercy of them; my second novel came out of that. I remember people saying that nothing ever happened to anyone in Iowa City and me wondering what in the world they were talking about. I remember, above all, during the three and a half years I lived in Iowa City, believing that what mattered more than anything else in your life was writing as well as you possibly could.

The University of Iowa field house was built in 1927 with metal and brick and a very low ceiling to create beautifully bad acoustics. The chairs were packed close together on top of the court, and the balcony seats were all benches: When one person cheered, this cheer flowed into the blood stream of the person next to you and you got a cumulative effect. Every sound echoed and re-echoed; every ovation was shared with your neighbor. On the north and south sides, steel support beams restricted vision for fifty years. (A new building went up in the early '80s.)

The speech clinic, by contrast, had brightly colored carpeting, long echoing corridors, stone staircases, and room after room of one-way observation mirrors, mini-cams in the corner, cassette recorders on wooden desks, word-worried people in plastic chairs, clinicians with monogrammed coffee cups. The therapy rooms were visited primarily by three-year-old possessors of cleft palates and six-year-old lispers, so most of the chairs were tiny wooden structures and there were coloring books stacked on the undersized tables, plastic toys to play with on the carpet. At an absurdly small desk in absurdly small chairs, like double Gullivers among Lilliputian furniture, sat my therapist and I.

The audiovisual center of the clinic was one square room bound by glass walls and populated by closed circuit television screens. The image popped into place: my therapist, sweet but plain with her bleached face, short hair, white blouse, dark jeans; me, my hair tousled, my shirt sleeves so poorly rolled up as to resemble Elizabethan armlets, my head bent so low it was almost touching the tiny table. The new blackboard, untouched, glistened in the corner.

For all its gestures toward modernity, the field house could have been a Sioux City barn and as such urged community. The Speech and Hearing Clinic was Bauhaus, with its efficient demand for a livable life. The only requirement of a fan or a patient is the surrender to authority. I yearned to become both and, in my inability to identify absolutely with another boy's body or my own mouth, created lacunae only written words could cross: I became a writer.

How had my life come to this, I wondered, shuttling back and forth between two four-story brick buildings (the Writers' Workshop, the Speech Clinic), two houses of language?

There are many novels, such as *Billy Budd, The Horse's Mouth, One Flew Over the Cuckoo's Nest,* and *The World According to Garp,* that feature characters who stutter, but my novel *Dead Languages* is, to my knowledge, the only one that takes as its principal subject the experience of stuttering. I wanted to convey exactly what it felt like to stutter, to communicate the agony of incommunication. To be locked inside one's own dead language and vainly strive to articulate one's full essence: This, to me, is not only a fair summary of my fictional alter ego Jeremy Zorn's particular predicament but the very definition of being human and especially, perhaps, of being a child, whose powerlessness, isolation, and narcissism—combined with a fierce need to communicate these states—are only the more manifest, transparent versions of what an adult feels.

I was a patient in the Speech Clinic for five years; the therapy I received there has had an enormous, lasting benefit upon my speech. However, when writing the book, I knew I needed to get out from under the technical terminology of speech therapy. And yet I also hoped to avoid the bathos of a disease-of-the-week TV movie. What I wanted was the sound of an adult Jeremy writing at precisely the same time as the child Jeremy was stuttering. I wanted the sound of literature glossing life while life was exploding the sound of literature. Through insistent, at times obsessional alliteration, I hoped to bring together simultaneously the lyricism of Jeremy the writer and the anguish of Jeremy the stutterer. And who is Jeremy to me, or I to Jeremy? He is the more manifest, transparent version: smarter, more confused, crueler, sweeter, more serious, funnier, more disfluent, more desperate, both my best and worst self—a hyperrealized self.

At age eleven, Jeremy tries to read John Updike's novel *Rabbit, Run;* only much later does he come to think that Updike built such ornate syntax as triumph over his own stutter. Jeremy resents it when his high school teacher equates Somerset Maugham's somewhat clumsy literary style with Maugham's stutter; Jeremy wants gorgeous written language to be a revenge upon the Babel of his spoken language. Somewhere within the world of words, he needs—he realizes—to succeed hysterically. Whether or not the novel succeeds is not, of course, for me to determine. What's interesting to me now, though, is how absolutely *Dead Languages* mattered to me when I was writing it. Not only was it an extremely autobiographical novel about growing up but an extremely autobiographical novel about growing up via language, and thus I felt this was my one and last chance to get it right: to go from stuttering child to storytelling adult.

Since writing may well be Jeremy's one chance to win, he overvalues written language. It's precisely this overvaluation of written language, though, that prevents him from ever entirely losing self-consciousness, as a writer and a person, when conveying his feelings. The pervasive alliteration in the book serves as metaphor for both the transformation of the wounds of childhood into the bow of art and for the incapacity of anyone to transform these wounds into anything but scar tissue.

Although I certainly still stutter, I've gained sufficient control of my speech that I feel perfectly comfortable teaching and lecturing, giving readings and doing interviews. From time to time I see a speech therapist for a quick refresher, but I'm done with disfluency—bored with it as label and trope. I have no more to say about it that I haven't already said in the book. Or so I tell myself until I experience a severe stuttering block and feel five years old again, from my tongue to my toes.

Letter to My Father

—⁓—

Dear Dad,

After our phone conversation last night—in which you said, apropos of *Dead Languages* and the "uncomfortably close" resemblance between yourself and the character of Teddy, that your pride in my accomplishment was at least matched by your anger and shame at seeing your foibles publicly paraded—I thought I would sit down and try to write to you some of my thoughts and feelings about the relationship between "real life" and fiction. Your response to all of the following may only be (though I hope it isn't): "Methinks he doth protest too much."

Any novel, no matter how autobiographical (and mine certainly looks plenty so), is a verbal machine that wants only to function, and the writer will do everything he can to get the book to work.

More specifically, it seems to me that a writer uses a combination of characteristics from different characters or character types—based on memory, imagination, available archetypes, and his own odd will—to create "characters," who are pieces of language that the author wants to work together in a way that makes a meaningful puzzle. "Yeah, yeah," I'm sure you're thinking, "but how would he like it if I wrote a book in which all *his* most embarrassing moments had been resurrected for all to see?"

One of the things I've learned about writing a novel is that once you get certain characters and certain relationships set up, it's virtually impossible to alter these relationships or change these characteristics in any significant way. Once you put a character on a particular path, e.g., Teddy suffers from bouts of manic depression, that's the sort of path he tends to follow throughout the book. The rhetoric, grammar, and coherence of the book demand that. I mean the portrait of Teddy (of "you") as a sympathetic one, and I hope that comes across—the ferocious identification and empathy between Jeremy and Teddy. Some of my favorite scenes in the book (Jeremy observing his father at the dinner party in the opening chapter, Jeremy buying his father a lime Sno-Cone, Jeremy going to Montbel to tell his father that Annette has died) are pretty much, so far as I can tell, love letters from me to you.

Novels, at least the ones that I seem to want to write and read, are about problems, failures, pain, and so when I wrote *Dead Languages*, the characters tended to take on the one most problematic quality of members of our family as I remember them from my childhood. The dominant trait of each character in the book—in some ways almost the only trait of each character in the book—is the one that stood most powerfully to me as the symbol or symptom of some sort of tension: my stuttering, your manic depression, Mom's obsession with political causes, Paula's struggles with her weight. (I don't suppose it's any solace that I feel I was much harder on myself than I was on anyone else? I got to control the disclosures.) The imagination—my imagination, in any case—feasts on one attribute, takes that one attribute, and can't let go. All good novels are about fully dimensional characters, and yet there is something, it seems to me, of the cartoon to all memorable characters in fiction.

Maybe I'm just not a good enough writer yet to create fully dimensional characters; maybe it takes an exceptionally talented or experienced or mature writer to create characters who are not only interesting but also not always pained—to show them in their happiness and fullness and glory, and yet not sentimentalize them, either. Maybe writers cartoonize what they can't fully understand.

I've tried to cut a subjective swath through my own patch of experience, as any writer must do, and I hope I haven't harmed anyone in the process, particularly you. Because this is a book about inconsolable pain, the portrait of Teddy leaves out many of the wonderful times and good moments and full feelings. I needn't tell you—or maybe I do, but certainly you must know—that I love you with all my heart and soul for all the support you've given me, all the nourishment and encouragement, all the laughs and discussions and insights, all the jokes and games and tears and tribulations, all the complicated, joyful, mysterious legacy handed down from father to son. If I didn't get all this into the book, it's because I'm not a good enough writer yet.

Love,
David

Games and Words and Ice

—⟋⟍—

Two of the things I love the most in the world—language and sports—my father taught me to love. I'm no longer much of an athlete at all. I have a bad back, tendinitis in my shoulder, a trick knee, I wear orthotics in my shoes to balance the unevenness of my legs, and I have a little pinch in my neck that's been bothering me lately, whereas at ninety my father's major ailment appears to be tennis elbow. He gets upset when it rains because that means he can only work out in the gym rather than speed-walk around the track and then work out in the gym. He speed-walks and swims every day. He still plays golf and, occasionally, tennis. He's the most vital person I've ever known.

On my tenth birthday, when my father was fifty-six, he pitched so hard to me and my friends that we were afraid to hit against him. "Get in the batter's box," he growled at us. One of my fondest memories is from about fifteen years ago—him and me sitting on his couch in the dark, listening to the radio broadcast of a Giants-Dodgers game; when Mike Marshall hit a three-run home run in the tenth inning to win it for the Dodgers, he and I looked at each other and we were both, a little weirdly, crying. From the time I was six years old, the first thing he and I have done every morning is read the sports page.

Games have held us together, but also words. I've always loved his love of puns, bad puns and worse puns; admired his ability to tell a joke and a story. He flew to Providence to attend my college graduation, and the day before the ceremony we went on a tour of John Brown House at the Rhode Island Historical Society. On and on the docent droned, giving us the official version of American history. My father and I tried not to laugh, but as we went from room to room, we were in an ecstasy of impudent giggles. "Subvert the dominant paradigm"—so goes the bumper sticker, which has passed now into cultural cliché. In so many ways, though, he showed me how to do exactly that: to not accept accepted wisdom, to insist on my own angle, to view language as a playground, and a playground as bliss. He showed me how to love being in my own body, how to love the words that emerged from my mouth and from my typewriter, how to love being myself and not some other self, and this self owes all of that to him.

I wrote this for my father's ninetieth birthday party, but loath to stutter before fifty of my father's cronies, I pocketed the speech and that night had a guilt-induced dream:

I open the front door to my father's house, and he has a slanted block of wood, the door stop, in his hand. He thinks I'm trying to break in. Without his glasses, in the unlit hallway, he thinks I'm a burglar. He's going to stop me with a 3" x 5" piece of wood. He squeezes the wood and gets a sliver in his palm, dropping the door stop on his shoes.

Tissues bulge out of each pocket of his bathrobe. Underneath, he's wearing khaki pants and a wool shirt. His hand is in his right pocket, jingling change.

Hello, he says.

It's good to see you, Father, I say, although I've never in my life called him "Father."

There's no light on in the house. It's four o'clock in February and I want a lamp, a candle, or a fire to take the cold off the walls and out of the wooden floors. The windows are shut and the shades are drawn.

Don't track dirty snow into the house, he says. Go shake your shoes off outside. (Growing up in California, I didn't see snow until I went east to college.)

Random walls of snowdrifts rise out of the field, and in the dismal sun the trees reflect onto the snow like huge, broken umbrellas. The wind sweeps the snow off the ground, through the trees, and against the windows of the house.

In the living room, he rocks in his chair, with his feet on the stool. His hands are folded in his lap. He opens his mouth, but no words come out. Newspapers are scattered across the floor. I sit away from him on the springs of a couch without cushions.

Under the glass tabletop next to him is a black-and-white picture of him hiking in the mountains with a walking stick in one hand, a pipe in the other. In the photograph, he has a backpack on and is half-turned toward the camera; in the photo, sunlight glamorizes his face.

I lift up the glass, hold up the picture by its edges, and place it in front of him.

Look at this picture, I say.

I need my glasses, he says.

You can see without them, I say.

It's fuzzy, he says. Get me my glasses.

A leather case is on the arm of the couch. I take out a pair of glasses that have sturdy black frames but no lenses. I hand the picture and glasses to him.

He can't hold the picture steady; his hands shake and stop and jerk again. I reach over from behind him and point to his face. The collar of his bathrobe is specked with dandruff.

Look at yourself, I say.

His glasses are too large and rest on the tip of his nose. He looks over the frames to study the picture.

I am, he says.

I took that picture; don't you remember?

No. Who is it?

You.

He puts his hand inside his bathrobe and, with his chin pressed to his chest, studies his shirt. When he tries to drop the photograph into the pocket of his bathrobe, the photo slips out of his hand and drifts to the floor.

I open the window shade. Outside, it's twilight. The wind snaps twigs off the tree limbs; twigs fall into the snow. The snow-drifts are higher now.

Is the walkway clear? he asks.

The walkway from the porch to the driveway to the street is two feet deep in snow.

No, Father, I say. Why?

Let's go for a walk.

It's five below.

Let's go to the post office.

You can't go out like that. You'll—

I'm expecting a letter, he says. Will you shovel the walkway?

At least change into something warmer.

The shovel's on the porch.

I stand deep in the snow and dig into the snowdrifts on either side of me. A sudden gust of wind and the weight of the shovel nearly make me fall. He stands behind the screen door, wearing a jacket so big he could use it as a sleeping bag. The pockets are at his knees and the hood is puffed out, framing his face.

There's ice on the walkway, he says.

I hit the blade against the ice, but it's frozen solid. He holds onto my arm and steps down off the porch, shuffling his feet until we get to the road, which is nearly a foot deep in snow. We trudge toward the post office at the end of the block. He holds onto my shoulder to prevent himself from falling.

Who wrote you a letter? I ask.

You did, he says.

I don't think so, I say. I think you have all my letters.

The post office is an old brick building. Its cement steps are covered with snow, and its wooden door is halfway off its hinges. Inside are benches and a warped floor and a couple of hundred post office boxes: rose-colored glass rectangles with black numbers.

He takes off his coat and uses it as a pillow, kneeling on the floor and turning the dials of a box, rattling it until it opens. He beats his right hand against the sides.

No letter, he says. Held up. Again.

Outside, the sky is blankly black, the color of my gloves. Too cold to move, he clings to my arm. Ice gathers on his hood, forming a comical cap. He stops to cough, closing his eyes and breathing heavily.

Are you all right? I ask.

I'm cold, he says.

The return trip is an exceedingly brief flash-forward. And there the dream ends.

III.

ME

Autobiography's Rapture

—ɷ—

THE OPENING SENTENCE of Nabokov's autobiography, *Speak, Memory*, is communal, contemplative: "The cradle rocks above an abyss, and common sense tells us that our existence is but a brief crack of light between two eternities of darkness." By contrast, the first line of his first English-language novel, *The Real Life of Sebastian Knight*—"Sebastian Knight was born on the thirty-first of December 1899, in the former capital of my country"—is concerned with the names, dates, and places of the world. In *Speak, Memory*, when Nabokov announces, "Toilers of the world, disband! Old books are wrong. The world was made on a Sunday," I simply assent, reveling in its praise of play, whereas when the same sentiment—"No, Leslie, I'm not dead. I have finished building a world, and this is my Sabbath rest"—appears

in *The Real Life of Sebastian Knight,* I read "through" it, interpret
it, treat it as a revelation not of truth but of personality.

Although *Speak, Memory* is chronological, it is in a sense
unplotted. It moves from one character, one city, to another
not on the basis of narrative but according to the movements of
memory. "The following of thematic designs through one's life
should be, I think, the true purpose of autobiography," Nabokov
writes. Transition from section to section is invariably triggered
by the process of memory: "With a sharp and merry blast from
the whistle that was part of my first sailor suit, my childhood
calls me back into that distant past to have me shake hands again
with my delightful teacher." Nabokov claims he's simply the
conduit of these recollections; memory's the active agent.

In *The Real Life of Sebastian Knight,* the movement from place
to place is accomplished according to the demands of, especially,
temporal progression. Most chapters open with a plotted move
forward in time: "Two years had elapsed after my mother's death
before I saw Sebastian again." No matter how traditional or
experimental a novel may be, the reader is meant to be struck
by its fulfillment or frustration of story; we expect autobiography, on the other hand, to be an examination of the process by
which it, and its author, came to be. It's easier for autobiography
to be about itself than fiction is, because by its very definition,
autobiography is concerned with the consciousness of its creator
in the process of creating a self. Autobiography appears to be
more tolerant than fiction is of sheer rapture, for if the novelist can deflect through drama the fact that "our existence is but
a brief crack of light between two eternities of darkness," the
autobiographer is allowed and even expected to surrender to the
unfathomable phenomenon that is his own life.

Satire

—꧂—

Satire is what closes Saturday night.
—George S. Kaufman

IN MY SENIOR year of high school, I was the editor of the school newspaper. Renée, who was the assistant editor, was determined to become the first girl or junior to edit the paper in the school's short and preferably forgotten history. As the outgoing editor, I recommended—actually, chose—my successor. Renée was aware of this.

The office itself was an odd mix of desolation and faux fashion. Renée thought I designed it that way, but in truth I never gave a second thought to the room's color scheme and furniture. A green chalkboard, with cracks down the middle, was nailed to the wall. A cork bulletin board framed the assignment sheet. I scribbled the story assignments in pencil, which smeared, so no one could read my writing and Renée and I could write all the articles. In one corner of the room, near the door, was an enormous black leather chair in which Renée always sat (with her platform shoes kicked under the chair, sweater draped across the head rest, bare feet tucked into the crevices). I don't remember her ever sitting in any other chair.

Late one night, in May—after the parking lots and swimming pools and playing fields were emptied—Renée and I were counting the newspapers to be distributed in the morning. We divided the 1,500 newspapers into sixty rolls, each of which we wrapped with a rubber band. Renée was moving her lips as she counted the papers. Helpfully, I pointed this out to her.

"You made me lose track," she said.

The late sun cast light into the room through the windows. Renée's face was faintly shadowed on the wall. The heater sputtered. The lights flickered, then died; I hit the wall and they came back on.

"It makes you look like a slow reader," I said.

"What?"

"Moving your lips makes you look like a slow reader."

"It's just a habit."

"I know, but if you want to be editor next year . . ." Power corrupts; absolute power, etc.

I counted sloppily and probably inaccurately while Renée continued to whisper numbers to herself, intermittently licking the forefinger of her right hand. I suddenly began counting aloud in Latin, with great seriousness, as if I were chanting Mass.

"Stop it," she said. "Please."

"It shouldn't bother you. If you want to be editor next year, you can't let little things bother you."

"Enough about—"

"Anyway, I thought you were taking Latin."

"But I can't think in Latin or try to count in English while you're counting in Latin. I mean, I'm only in second year."

"Do you prefer Horace or Juvenal?" I asked.

"What do you mean?"

"Haven't you been reading any Horace or Juvenal?"

She played with a rubber band, stretching it until it snapped. "Just sentences here and there," she said.

"Well, whom do you prefer?"

"I don't know. They're both all right. What's the difference?"

She made me feel much older than I actually was. Not even little children made me feel as lifeless as Renée did. Her loyalty was to questions and mine, sadly, was to answers. But the difference between Horace and Juvenal meant, at that time, everything to me. I wanted desperately for her to see and feel, quite like nothing else, this difference. I had, in fact, waited all year to illustrate this very thing to her, and I got up from my chair and stood over her. She responded, quite naturally, by putting her feet out as a barrier.

"They were both satirists," I said, stepping back. "I was the only person in the class who liked Juvenal. I love Juvenal. Horace loved the people he wrote about, but Juvenal couldn't. The poor man hated everybody."

"You're terrible. Juvenal must have hated himself."

"Even greater consistency!"

"I pity you, I really do."

"Pity won't get you the editorship."

Renée's folders and books were on the table. The Latin book

I had studied two years earlier was on top. The cover showed a Roman soldier's profile against a green background. The lettering was orange. Toward the bottom of the front cover was written *Laudatus sum:* I have been praised. I did not want to be praised. I did not want to praise anyone else. I was not worth praising. Neither was anyone else. I did not want to write constructive editorials.

Renée had attached paper clips to many pages and highlighted important rules in pink. The margins of the pages were filled with questions and reminders and doodles she had written to herself. Her handwriting was sweeping, immaculate, breathless.

"How far are you?" I asked, turning the pages of her book, trying to find a certain sentence of Juvenal's.

"I've counted out all but the senior homerooms."

"I mean, how far are you in Latin?"

"Third conjugation verbs."

"This verb's third conjugation," I said, handing the book to her and pointing to the Juvenal quotation.

Renée put the book down on the chair and mouthed the words to herself. Then she read it aloud, slowly, awkwardly, pronouncing the words as if they were Spanish. "'*Difficile est saturam non scribere.*' That's easy," she said. "It is not difficult to write satire."

"Close."

"Difficult satire is not to be written."

I shook my head.

She curled her hair behind her ears. "Satire is not written difficultly."

I shook my head again.

"It is satire which is difficult to write for nobody." It was such a short sentence, but she still didn't seem to get Juvenal's sentiment. I laughed a little—what an asshole.

"What, then?"

"It's difficult *not* to write satire."

"What?"

"Don't you see? Juvenal found it difficult to do anything but write satire. Horace probably could have written anything but only decided now and then to write satire. Juvenal had to. He had no choice."

"Well, what's so great about doing what comes naturally?"

"Juvenal didn't rein in any of his hate. He despised the fools around him. He refused to love them. He simply couldn't. I love him."

A drop of sweat from Renée's forehead spilled onto her lips. She rubbed her hand on her face, streaking newsprint across her cheek, then she straddled the chair and stood up, tipping over the small stack of newspapers which remained. On her tiptoes, in her bare feet, she pulled down the camera case from the cabinet. The lights went out and she banged the wall to get them to stay on. She took the lens cap off and fidgeted with the dials. I was supposedly somewhat photogenic as a teenager, and yet I disliked quite a lot being photographed. Renée knew this, knew I couldn't stand the pseudo-truth of a "candid" portrait. She attached the flash, pressed her nose to the back of the camera, and pointed it at me, then pressed the button.

I still have the photograph, and what's striking to me now about it is its amazing generosity. I hadn't ever been particularly nice to Renée, but the picture—a sort of out-of-focus X ray of my eyes—shows how badly I wanted to learn how to love her. It shows this while refusing to judge it one way or another. Although of course I couldn't hear it in time to do anything about it because I wasn't listening, I had been praised.

Rebecca's Journal

—⁓—

FROM THE SOUND of things, the girl who lived next door to me my sophomore year of college was having problems with her boyfriend. One night Rebecca invited me into her room to share a joint and told me she kept a journal, which one day she hoped to turn into a novel. I said that Kafka believed that writing in a journal prevented reality from being turned into fiction, but as she pointed out, Kafka did nothing if not write in a journal. I liked the way she threw her head back when she laughed.

The next day I knocked on her door to ask her to join me for lunch. Her door was unlocked; she assumed no one would break into her room and, in any case, the door to the dormitory was always locked. Rebecca wasn't in and neither was her roommate, who had all but moved in to her boyfriend's apartment off campus. Rebecca's classes weren't over until late afternoon, I remembered, and I walked in and looked at her clothes and books and notebooks. Sitting down at her desk, I opened the bottom right drawer and came across a photo album, which I paged through only briefly, because underneath the album was a stack of Rebecca's journals. The one on top seemed pretty current and I started reading: The past summer, she missed Gordon terribly and let herself be used on lonely nights by a Chapel Hill boy whom she had always fantasized about and who stroked her hair in the moonlight and wiped himself off with leaves. When Rebecca returned to Providence in the fall, she knew she wanted romance, and after weeks of fights that went all night and into the morning, she told Gordon she didn't want to see him anymore.

Me, on the other hand, she wanted to see every waking moment of the day and night. As a stutterer, I was even more ferociously dedicated to literature (the glory of language that was beautiful and written) than other English majors at Brown were, and I could turn up the lit-crit rhetoric pretty damn high. She loved the way I talked (my stutter was endearing); her favorite thing in the world was to listen to me rhapsodize about John Donne. She often played scratchy records on her little turntable (this was 1975), and when I said, "The *Jupiter Symphony* might be the happiest moment in human history," her heart skipped a beat. Toward my body she was ambivalent: She was simultaneously attracted and repelled by my strength. She was afraid I might crush her. These are, I swear, near-verbatim quotes.

I finished reading the journal and put it away, then went back to my room and waited for Rebecca to return from her classes. That night we drove out to Newport, where we walked barefoot in the clammy sand and looked up at the lighted mansions that lined the shore in the distance. "The rich, too, must go to sleep at night," I said, offering Solomonic wisdom. We stood atop a ragged rock that sat on the shoreline; the full tide splashed at our feet. The moon made halos of our heads. I put my hands through her hair and kissed her lightly on the lips. "Don't kiss hard," she said. "I'm afraid I'll fall."

Tuesday and Thursday afternoons—when she worked in the development office—I'd go into her room, shut the door, lock it, and sit back in the swivel chair at her desk. She always left a window open. The late fall wind would be blowing the curtains around, and the *Jupiter Symphony* would always be on the little red record player on the floor. She often left wet shirts hanging all over the room and they'd ripple in the wind eerily. On the floor were cracked pots of dead plants. On the wall were a few calligraphic renderings of her own poetry. Her desk was always a mess, but her journal—a thick black book—was never very difficult to find.

I was nineteen years old and a virgin and at first I read Rebecca's journal because I needed to know what to do next and what she liked to hear. Every little gesture, every minor movement I made she passionately described and wholeheartedly admired. When we were kissing or swimming or walking down the street, I could hardly wait to rush back to her room to find out what phrase or what twist of my body had been lauded in her journal. I loved her impatient handwriting, her purple ink, the melodrama of the whole thing. It was such a surprising and addictive respite, seeing every aspect of my being celebrated by someone else rather than excoriated by myself. She wrote, "I've never truly loved anyone the way I love D. and it's never been so total and complete, yet so unpossessing and pure, and sometimes I want to drink him in like golden water." *You* try to concentrate on your Milton midterm after reading that about yourself.

Sometimes, wearing her bathrobe, she'd knock on my door in order to return a book or get my reaction to a paragraph she'd written or read. She'd say, "Goodnight," turn away from me, and begin walking back to her room. I'd call to her, and we'd embrace—first in the hallway outside our doors, then soon enough in my room, her room, on our beds. I hadn't kissed a girl since I was twelve, so I tried to make up for lost time by swallowing Rebecca alive: biting her lips until they bled, licking her face, chewing on her ears, holding her up in the air and squeezing her until she screamed.

In her journal, she wrote that she'd never been kissed like this in her life and that she inevitably had trouble going to sleep after seeing me. I'd yank the belt to her bathrobe and urge her under the covers, but she refused. She actually said she was afraid she'd go blind when I entered her. Where did she learn these lines, anyway?

Shortly before the weather turned permanently cold, we went hiking in the mountains. The first night, she put her backpack at the foot of her sleeping bag—we kissed softly for a few minutes, then she fell asleep—but on the second night she put her backpack under her head as a pillow. Staring into the blankly black sky, I dug my fingers into the dirt behind Rebecca's head and, the first time and the second time and the third time and the fourth time and probably the twenty-fourth time, came nearly immediately.

From then on, I couldn't bring myself to read what she had written. I had read the results of a survey in which forty percent of Italian women acknowledged that they usually faked orgasms. Rebecca wasn't Italian—she was that interesting anomaly, a Southern Jew—but she thrashed around a lot and moaned and screamed and if she was pretending I didn't want to know about it. She often said that it had never been like this before.

Every night she'd wrap her legs around me and scream something that I thought was German until I realized she was saying, "Oh, my son." *My son?* She had her own issues, too, I suppose. We turned up the *Jupiter Symphony* all the way and attempted to pace ourselves so we'd correspond to the crashing crescendo. I was sitting on top of her and in her mouth, staring at her blue wall, and I thought *my whole body is turning electric blue.* She was on top of me, rotating her hips and crying, and she said, "Stop." I said, "Stop?" and stopped. She grabbed the back of my hair and said, "Stop? Are you kidding? Don't stop."

By the end of the semester, though, packing to fly home to San Francisco to spend the Christmas vacation with my family, I suddenly started to feel guilty about having read Rebecca's journal. Every time I kissed her, I closed my eyes and saw myself sitting at her desk, turning pages. I regretted having done it and yet I couldn't tell her about it.

"What's wrong?" she asked.

"I'll miss you," I said. "I don't want to leave."

On the plane I wrote her a long letter in which I told her everything I couldn't bring myself to tell her in person: that I had read her journal, that I was very sorry, that I thought that our love was still pure and we could still be together, but that I'd understand if she went back to Gordon and never spoke to me again.

She wrote back that I should never have depended on her journal to give me strength, that she would throw it away and never write in it again, and that she wanted to absolve me, but that she wasn't God, although she loved me better than God could. Anything I said she would believe because she knew that I would never lie to her again. She loved me, she said; she'd known and loved me all her life, but she had just now found me. Our love, in her view, transcended time and place.

Well, sad to say, it didn't. The night I returned from San Francisco, she left a note on my door that said only "Come to me," and we tried to imitate the wild abandon of the fall semester, but what a couple of weeks before was utterly instinctive was now excruciatingly self-conscious and the relationship quickly cooled. She even went back to Gordon for a while, though that second act didn't last very long, either.

It was, I see now, exceedingly odd behavior on my part. After ruining things for myself by reading her journal, I made sure I ruined things for both of us by telling her that I had read her journal. Why couldn't I just live with the knowledge and let the shame dissipate over time? What was—what is—the matter with me? Do I just have a bigger self-destruct button, and like to push it harder and more incessantly, than everyone else? True, but also the language of the events was at least as erotic to me as the events themselves, and when I was no longer reading her words, I was no longer very adamantly in love with Rebecca. This is what is known as a tragic flaw.

IV.

ME AS YOU

Using Myself

—ᴍ—

Many writers pretend that they don't read reviews of their books and that, in particular, life is too short to subject themselves to reading bad reviews. Kingsley Amis said that a bad review may spoil breakfast but you shouldn't allow it to spoil lunch. Jean Cocteau suggested, "Listen carefully to first criticisms of your work. Note carefully just what it is about your work that the critics don't like—then cultivate it. That's the part of your work that's individual and worth keeping."

Sane advice; I don't follow it. I read all my reviews, though not necessarily every word of every one of them. The really positive ones are boring after a while—your own most generous self-appraisal quoted back to yourself—but I must admit I find bad reviews fascinating. They're like the proverbial train wreck, only you're in the train; will all those mangled bodies at the bottom of the ravine tell you something unexpected about yourself?

Recently—as an experiment, I suppose, in psychic survival—I reread every horrific review that I've ever received, to see what I would learn. This is what I learned: I'm right. They're wrong. (Smiley face.) It was a genuinely odd, and in a way, riveting experience, the hour or so it took me to read bad reviews of five books. I felt as if I were locked in a room, getting worked over by a dozen, supposedly well-meaning guidance counselors. Suddenly my body felt like it had gotten filled with liquid cement.

One otherwise fairly positive review of my novel *Dead Languages* concluded, "The novel as a whole doesn't quite uncurl from its fetal position, doesn't open out from self-conscious-ness toward reconciliation." A reviewer of my novel-in-stories, *Handbook for Drowning,* said about the book's protagonist, "The smudged eye turns into the eye that smudges what it sees. Clinging to the child role of bearing witness to itself, it doesn't undertake the adult role of bearing witness to everything else. Cramped, Walter tells a cramped story. The glimpses we see, varied and subtle as they may be, are all gray. It is the grayness of life seen through a caul that has never been shed." My first reaction, when I reread these reviews, was to think, "You know, they're right. I must figure out how to open out from self-con-sciousness toward reconciliation. I must undertake the adult role of bearing witness to everything else." But then I realized that I don't do reconciliation. I don't do witness to everything else. Sorry. Nabokov said, "I do not know if it has ever been noted before that one of the main characteristics of life is discreteness. Unless a film of flesh envelops us, we die. Man exists only insofar as he is separated from his surroundings. The cranium is a space-traveler's helmet. Stay inside or you perish. Death is divestment, death is communion. It may be wonderful to mix with the landscape, but to do so is the end of the tender ego." I think of my work as being relentlessly loyal to this existential truth, whereas one reviewer of my most recent book, *Black Planet,* called it the "wretched musings of one white guy with a panicky ego, a pitiable heart, and too much time on his hands."

"Pitiable heart" interests me, as does this judgment about the same book: "At least it should make some white readers feel good about themselves. They may be screwed up about race, but they're not as annoyingly screwed up as David Shields." The impulse on reviewers' part to use me to get well—to brandish their own more evolved morality, psyche, humanity—flies in the face of what is to me an essential assumption of the compact between reader and writer, especially between the reader and writer of autobiography: Doesn't everybody have a pitiable heart? Aren't we all Bozos on this bus? Robert Dana explains it like this:

> Was Keats a confessional poet? When he talks about youth that grows 'pale and spectre-thin, and dies,' he's talking about his kid brother, Tom, who died of tuberculosis. But he's talking about more than that. The word 'confessional' implies the need to purge oneself and go receive forgiveness for one's life. I don't think that's what confessional poetry is about at all. I think it's a poetry that comes out of the stuff of the poet's personal life, but he's trying to

render this experience in more general and inclusive, or
what used to be called 'universal,' terms. He's presenting
himself as a representative human being. He's saying, 'This
is what happens to us because we're human beings in this
human world, this flawed and difficult world where joy
is rare.' Sylvia Plath is certainly one of the outstanding
'confessional' poets, but when she entitles a poem 'Lady
Lazarus,' she's trying to connect herself to the whole tradition of pain and death and resurrection. She's not presenting herself as Sylvia Plath, but as a part of a larger pattern.
A more grotesque manifestation of it.

My shtick, exactly. When I present myself as a "tube boob" (one
review) in *Remote* or as a "pathetically guilty white liberal" (another review) in *Black Planet,* I mean for "David Shields" to be
a highly stylized representative through whom cultural energies
and all manner of mad human needs flow.

When one reviewer says about *Remote,* "The futuristically
formless nature of the collection gets irritating; it's an ambivalent comment on bookmaking, and before long it's got us feeling
ambivalent, too," or another reviewer says about the same book,
"The danger, of course, in writing about fluff and modern life is
that you spend too much time thinking about fluff and modern
life, until you resemble not a little the prostitutes in *You'll Never
Make Love in This Town Again,* trapped, mired, in it," I understand the comments are meant as dispraise, but if you're feeling
ambivalent about it, that's a good thing; if I seem to you to be
trapped, mired in it, that's the point. Theodor Adorno says that
a "successful work is not one which resolves objective contradic-

tions in a spurious harmony, but one which expresses the idea of harmony negatively by embodying the contradictions, pure and uncompromised, in its innermost structure." Exactly what I'm always seeking to do: embody the contradictions.

A reviewer of *Remote* said, "Shields wouldn't thank anyone who suggested, on the basis of the material presented in this book, that as the child of 'Jewish liberal activists,' he might have chosen passivism as the subtlest form of rebellion." Why would the reviewer think I included this information, unless I wanted readers to make precisely this kind of connection? If via my pitiable heart the reader intuits something about his own, that, to me, is a worthwhile trade-off. What a guy, what a guy. This *Remote* reviewer concluded by mentioning a relatively minor misdeed I acknowledged committing, and then said, "Presumably, by now we're past the stage of being expected to say, 'Hell, we've all done that.'" Not done that—imagined that. Goethe said, "I've never heard of a crime which I could not imagine committing myself." To me, it's almost unfathomable that a reviewer would say, as one did about *Black Planet*, "The author escapes the morass of self-doubt as so many others do—by vicarious identification with a professional athlete; Shields idolizes Sonics player Gary Payton to the point of unnerving fixation," and then not figure that I'm up to something other than chronicling my own fandom. Another reviewer of *Black Planet* asked, "Do we really need to know what David Shields is fantasizing about when he's having sex? Does he imagine his foibles are our own?" I'm certain my foibles are your own, if only you're willing to acknowledge them. "A man's life of any worth is a continual allegory," said Keats, who should know.

The Same Air

—⟋⟍—

I SPENT PRETTY much the entire 1970s indoors. As the indefatigable editor of my high school newspaper, I wrote innumerable editorials in bold support of the ecology club. In college, I took curious pride in being the last person to leave the library nearly every night for four years. In graduate school at the University of Iowa, I hammered typewriter keys so incessantly that the landlord had trouble keeping the apartment directly below mine rented.

Rachel, whom I met in grad school, and I left Iowa City shortly after Ronald Reagan's inauguration in 1981 to move to Los Angeles, where we lived for a few months with her parents in their glass house overlooking the ocean. Rachel's father was a movie producer, and the first week we were in LA we went to a party in Malibu Colony at Walter Matthau's house. Someone asked me what I did and I said I was a writer and she asked me what I was writing and I said a novel and she said, quite curtly, "Oh, you mean a pre-movie."

An odd mixture of people showed up at Rachel's parents' house: Oona Chaplin, Jean Stapleton, Henry Winkler. Rachel's mother and stepfather and stepsister were beautiful in a way that neither Rachel nor I was. In a menagerie of priceless objects, we weren't priceless objects, which caused me to feel so self-conscious and nervous that for the first and only time in my life I developed high blood pressure. A semifamous actress actually said to Rachel that Rachel reminded her of Rachel's dog in that physically they weren't out of the ordinary but that once you got to know both of them you really admired their unique spirits.

Hundred-dollar haircuts newly failed to strike me as hilarious. Dermabrasion and rhinoplasty didn't seem prima facie evidence of self-hatred. I got contact lenses. Rachel got such a flattering haircut that her mother made her promise on the spot that wherever she lived the rest of her life she'd fly back once a month and get her hair cut the same way by the same person.

Rachel's parents somehow managed to make watching TV seem to be a glamorous and vital and also slightly outré activity. When Rachel and I weren't driving into Beverly Hills to go to premieres or into Westwood to see movies on the night they opened, we were watching TV or reading the *LA Times* or reading the trades or reading screenplays or teleplays. In grad school, I almost never read anything written after World War II; I now had trouble reading anything that hadn't been written in the last few weeks.

I was born in LA and am utterly uninterested in LA jokes. That's not what this is about. What this is about is this: Other people who had been less cloistered than I may have registered the shift a little earlier, and my sudden immersion in media- and celebrity-culture was so extreme as to constitute something like shock therapy, but for me, 1981 is the year America as we now know it became America as we now know it; 1981 is the year the world changed forever; 1981 is the year everyone suddenly started breathing the same air.

Remoteness

Even a few years ago, after clear weather, you couldn't see smog here for three days; now you can see it after one day. Eddie Bauer was once the brand name of choice, even for downtown businessmen; Tiffany's and Cartier are now in Pacific Place, Neiman Marcus in the Westlake Center. Everyone downtown seems to be wearing designer eyewear, Italian shoes, expensive leather coats. Late-model SUVs ("I'm in touch with nature") and Volvos ("I'm intellectual") are ubiquitous, though very few Mercedes or BMWs, at least in the neighborhoods where I drive. A friend who was a successful potter was forced to give up his studio when the rent doubled, so he's now remodeling houses for millionaires half his age. There are now 60,000 millionaires (one-third of whom are Microsoft employees or former employees) living in the Seattle area. A friend's former student, who received his MFA degree at Eastern Washington University several years ago, was divorced and destitute; his temp agency assigned him to the warehouse at Amazon—Jeff Bezos's garage. He's now worth $10 million (he cashed out before the stock plummeted).

The bidding for the house around the corner in my shabby-genteel neighborhood was between an Amazon couple and a Microsoft couple, started at $509K, and finished a week later at $550K, cash. This was right around when Bezos was named *Time*'s "Man of the Year," before venture capital streams dried up and dozens of dot-coms folded, before Judge Thomas Penfield Jackson ordered the breakup of Microsoft into two companies, before Boeing moved its headquarters to Chicago. Now, houses which would have sold in days are staying on the market for a month. A sign of the Seattle economic collapse to come? All of Seattle may be in denial, but a former Microsoft employee who now works for Amazon said, "Anxiety about Microsoft is bogus. The case is affecting no one, not even Microsoft employees. They're convinced the judge's decision will be overturned on appeal; an incredibly high percentage of his decisions have been overturned in the past. Sure, cyberfolks here have worries— about the stock market in general, about employee retention. But Microsoft? Nah. That's the stablest thing around, no matter what shape it takes. It's old guard by now, like a rock."

■

Being a writer in image-addicted America makes me feel at times somewhat marginal; being a writer in cyber-sick Seattle often makes me feel absolutely beside the point. I was born in Los Angeles (the suburbs), grew up in San Francisco (the suburbs), went to college in Providence (where I rarely left College Hill) and graduate school in Iowa City, lived for a few years in New York, spent an alarming portion of my twenties sequestered in artists' colonies, taught at a small school in a tiny hamlet in upstate New York for three years, and so when I moved to Seattle in 1988 to take a teaching job in the creative writing program at the University of Washington, I thought of Seattle not as an idyll but as a real city. A small city but a real city, nonetheless.

Publicly, I condescended to Seattle, repeated the jokes ("When it's 11 PM in New York, it's 1972 in Seattle"), but privately I rather liked the containable snugness of Seattle. Publicly, I said it didn't matter anymore where one lived, but privately (quite unconsciously) I must have registered the remoteness of my new address, for in the last decade I've gone from being primarily a writer of novels and short stories to primarily a writer of nonfiction books and personal essays. (Never mind, for the moment, that I don't of course believe in the validity of these generic distinctions.) It was as if, upon arriving here, I no longer entirely trusted the life I lived on a daily level—the material of fiction, at least the sort of autobiographical fiction I write—to be of sufficient interest to people living east of the Cascade Mountains and so my work became saturated with overtly public, "nationwide" topics such as the psychodynamics of mass media, our love-hate relationship with celebrity, the racial subtext of professional basketball, etc.

This remoteness is a crucial part of the answer to the question people so often ask, "Why Seattle?"—i.e., how could such a sleepy fishing village become home to so many world-conquering companies? It's quite striking to me how many of the most successful businesses here—Boeing, Microsoft, Amazon, McCaw Cellular, Paccar (Peterbilt and Kenworth trucks), UPS (which began in Seattle as a cooperative)—have created products that have the specific effect of shrinking the distance between Seattle and the rest of the country. The very remoteness of Seattle engenders the need, which creates the imagination to fill the need. (There's a proverb about this.) This doesn't happen if you're living in Montclair, New Jersey, where you think you're living in or near the center of the universe. "The locus of innovation has shifted westward in the United States," as the chairman of the San Francisco Museum of Modern Art recently said. Or as my friend Joel likes to say, "The silicon chip wasn't invented in New York; it couldn't have been."

■

A few years ago Fred Moody, the former editor of the *Seattle Weekly*, wrote an article about a BBC film crew that came to Seattle to document what they assumed would be a vibrant city and wound up packing up its equipment and going home without much of a movie because they couldn't find the vibrancy anywhere. To Moody, the film crew didn't get Seattle. They didn't see that the bland face Seattle shows to the rest of world is a workaholic's "Do Not Disturb" sign. (I feel like my self-presentation is not entirely dissimilar to Seattle's in this regard.) Less politely, *Leave us the fuck alone*. (Ditto.) It's a Northern city—Scandinavian, Calvinist, Puritan—and a Pacific Rim city—Asian, self-effacing, "polite"—and a Western port city—blue-collar, hardworking, unshowy.

Moody recently told me, "Whenever I think about all this, I think about it as a native who grew up in a much more marvelous Seattle that disdained the kind of status-seeking that is endemic here now. It's hard to remember, but most of these hugely successful companies began as 'idealistic' enterprises of one kind or another. The three founders of Starbucks just wanted to make Seattle more like Italy—with these little coffee shops where people would sit around and discuss opera over espresso. Gordon Bowker, one of the Starbucks founders, is appalled by what the company has become. People forget that Microsoft was essentially a revolutionary guerrilla company intent on wresting computing power away from corporations and giving it to citizens"—a view Judge Jackson apparently didn't share. "They also forget that it was founded by teenagers. A lot of early Microsoft people feel tremendous discomfiture over how rich they got. No one ever dreamed anything like what happened would happen.

"I was walking around downtown during the WTO riots, and I was struck by how deep the resentment ran against the newly rich and technologically evangelistic in this huge population. (I was also struck, though, by how cell phone technology had made the protesters so much more powerful and effective and efficient.) But the more paradoxical thought was that with all the pretensions to sophistication and worldliness Seattle has taken on in recent years—a function of its rise in wealth and the power of Microsoft—it still is a small town, with a small-towner's inability to understand the real world. How else to explain the city's cluelessness in advance of these protests? Everyone in the world, practically, was trying to tell Seattle what would happen, but the city couldn't believe it because it lacked the imagination or the experience to even imagine being overrun."

A friend who's a Seattle real estate agent said, "All of the new rich (whom I've come to call NR) I've dealt with have been circumspect about discussing their financial gains. No one has boasted about their wealth; in fact, it has been the opposite." So Seattle. "I presented an offer to an NR couple in their early thirties who were selling. They were selling because they wanted to go to Paris to live for a few years." Yikes. "It was clear there was no job there. As we wrapped up the transaction, the NR wife asked that I please not tell the neighbors about their plan—to go to Paris." So embarrassing! "I live in the neighborhood, so she thought I might talk to one of our neighbors. I assured her I wouldn't. She went on to say, with a good deal of shyness, that she 'just didn't want to give . . . ' She didn't finish the sentence." As who could have? "But it was clear that she felt uncomfortable that they were young and retired, with money, and could make these incredible choices.

"I had another NR buyer last year who bought in Capitol Hill"—one of the most expensive neighborhoods of Seattle. "He didn't come from money and here he was, in his early forties, a rich man. As his agent, I needed to know what his financial plans were. He informed me he'd be paying cash. This didn't fall right out of his mouth. He didn't gloat or try to impress—just the opposite; he seemed uncomfortable admitting he had the means to do this. All cash. I told him he was fortunate. He said he never doubted it." What a genuinely graceful, utterly Seattle-esque answer.

Another Seattle native and longtime Seattle journalist, Bruce Barcott, now a writer for *Outside* magazine, said, "The 'Why don't we get the hell out of Seattle?' conversation has become a staple of my conversations with my wife. I blame the money, which has made it impossible to live in Seattle on anything less than an excellent salary and has, lastly and sadly, made Seattle into a worldwide center of ambition. In the 1980s and early 1990s the great thing about this place was that highly ambitious people went elsewhere—New York, DC, LA. In the early 1990s we received a culturally rich influx of twenty-somethings who moved here after high school or college to start up their own theater companies, paint, sculpt, dance, start a band, whatever. Seattle was a place you could just go and do your work and not worry about getting national reviews because they *weren't coming*. About five years ago we started getting another kind of immigrant—the hyperambitious money-smart set who see Seattle as a kind of junior varsity San Francisco. I date it from the moment Microsoft hired Michael Goff to run their ill-fated online 'channels.' Others date it from Michael Kinsley's hiring at *Slate*. That, and the weather's getting to me."

Barcott is right about the weather—it feels like it hasn't stopped raining since shortly after Kurt Cobain's suicide—but I don't know; is it really all that terrible if Seattle is now (or was, pre-Nasdaq crash) a "worldwide center of ambition"? Isn't that a good, or at least an amusing, thing? How relevant is it that the house which I "own" is worth more than twice what I paid for it in 1991? No, not "greed is good," but who wants to be too content where one lives? Isn't the Chinese curse "May you live in interesting times" also supposed to be a blessing? As British writer Jonathan Raban, another Seattle resident, once said, "I don't think you're supposed to exactly like where you live. I think you're supposed to *live* where you live, in a state of grumbling dissatisfaction with it."

A couple of years ago *Vanity Fair* ran a long article making fun of the way several former Microsoft employees were spending their millions—going hang gliding, opening flower shops, undertaking do-gooder projects. The rhetoric of the piece had to do with the way in which the East is supposedly about work and the West is supposedly about play. This is a fairy tale the East tells itself, as Hollywood and Silicon Valley and Redmond have colonized the world. "Reality," Jeff Bezos said at the height of his Midas mode, "is an interesting environment." Reality has recently become a considerably more interesting environment for Jeff Bezos, but when he initially said it, the great thing about the line was that no one could tell, exactly, whether he was kidding.

There is, to me, something fundamentally boring about money in the East. It maintains status quo, is about the past, just keeps feathering the nests of the patriarchs and their broods on Park Avenue and in Summit, New Jersey, and Ridgefield, Connecticut. Money in the West is about dreaming the golden dream—fantasies of the frontier, illusions of a new world to come. To people here, I'm a satirist of the city. In my two most recent books, *Remote* and *Black Planet,* I made fun of Seattle's upbeat earnestness. But, really, I love illusions of a new world to come; I don't see how anyone can live life without them. As difficult as I sometimes find to admit it, I'm a Westerner and even,

now, a Seattleite. I love being a resident of a remote state, disconnected to everyone else and therefore forced to make everything
up on our own, with the feverish hope that what we come up
with will somehow, magically, prove to be indispensable to the
rest of the world which, hemmed in by tradition, hadn't thought
of that yet.

V.

ME AND YOU

In Praise of Collage

—⁓𝍠⁓—

WHAT IN THE novel are character and plot are supplanted, in a work of literary collage, by theme and idea. For me, the considerable excitement of collage resides in watching the writer weave many separate strands into a beautiful, unbreakable braid.

▪

Renata Adler's *Speedboat* consists of hundreds of discrete, free-standing, seemingly unrelated paragraphs. Some of the episodes consist of only a couple of sentences; others are five pages long; most are about half a page. The book is an education in Adler's astringent sensibility, her brutal intelligence. We read her scenes not only to find out what will happen but also to see if we understand yet what, in Adler's view, constitute the crucial thematic elements of a scene. She repeats the schema over and over until she's taught the reader how to think about a certain nexus of concerns the same way she does: language, culture, politics, media, travel, technology are all different kinds of "speedboats"—exciting, unpredictable, powerful, and dangerous in their violent velocity. And just when we've grasped it, the book is over: "It could be that the sort of sentence one wants right here is the kind that runs, and laughs, and slides, and stops right on a dime."

Like *Speedboat,* George W.S. Trow's *Within the Context of No Context* is an assemblage of disconnected paragraphs, narrated in a tone of equally elaborate irony, and perhaps best understood as what Trow calls "cultural autobiography." In other words, its ostensible accomplishment—a brilliantly original analysis of the underlying grammar of mass culture—is a way for Trow to get at what is in one sense his ultimate subject: the difference between the world he inhabits (no context) and the world his father, a newspaperman, inhabited (context).

In the book's final paragraph, Trow writes: "Certainly, he [Trow's father] said, at the end of boyhood, when as a young man I would go on the New Haven railroad to New York City, it would be necessary for me to wear a fedora hat. I have, in fact, worn a fedora hat, but ironically. Irony has seeped into the felt of any fedora hat I have ever owned—not out of any wish of mine but out of necessity. A fedora hat worn by me without the necessary protective irony would eat through my head and kill me."

■

The first piece in Bernard Cooper's *Maps to Anywhere* was selected by Annie Dillard as one of the best essays of 1988, but the book as a whole won the PEN/Hemingway Award for the best first novel of 1990, while in the foreword to the book Richard Howard calls the chapters "neither fictions nor essays, neither autobiographical illuminations nor cultural inventions." The narrator—Howard calls him "the Bernard-figure (like the Marcel-figure, neither character nor symbol)"—is simultaneously "the author" and a fictional creation.

From mini-section to mini-section and chapter to chapter, Bernard's self-conscious and seriocomic attempts to evoke and discuss his own homosexuality, his brother's death, his father's failing health, his parents' divorce, and Southern California kitsch are delicately woven together to form an extremely powerful meditation on the relationship between grief and imagination. "Maps to anywhere" comes to mean: When a self can (through language, memory, research, and invention) project itself everywhere, and can empathize with anyone or anything, what exactly is a self? The book's final sentence—perfect final sentences seem particularly important to achieving closure in collage—is an articulation of the melancholy that the narrator has, to a degree, deflected until then: "And I walked and walked to hush the world, leaving silence like spoor."

■

Douglas Coupland's *Generation X* is, like *Maps to Anywhere,* set in Southern California, but Coupland is fifteen years younger than Cooper, and the texture of their books is extremely different. Graphics, statistics, and mock-sociological definitions compete, as marginalia, with the principal text, which consists of "tales" only loosely connected by the same cast of characters, but very tightly organized around the inability of any of the characters to feel, really, anything. The mixture of nonfiction and fiction—information crowding out imagination—in *Generation X* effectively embodies the idea that these characters, bombarded by mall culture and media, feel that they have "McLives" rather than lives.

■

Eduardo Galeano's *The Book of Embraces,* like *Speedboat* and *Within the Context of No Context,* consists of hundreds of extremely short sections; like *Maps to Anywhere,* it's an ode to the creative imagination's empathetic embrace of everything. A mix of memoir, anecdote, polemic, parable, fantasy, and Galeano's surreal drawings, the book might at first glance be dismissed as mere miscellany, but upon more careful inspection, *The Book of Embraces* reveals itself to be virtually a geometric proof on the themes of love, terror, and imagination, perhaps best exemplified in this extraordinarily compressed mini-chapter:

> Tracey Hill was a child in a Connecticut town who amused herself as befitted a child of her age, like any other tender little angel of God in the state of Connecticut or anywhere else on this planet.
> One day, together with her little school companions, Tracey started throwing lighted matches into an anthill.

They all enjoyed this healthy childish diversion. Tracey, however, saw something which the others didn't see or pretended not to, but which paralyzed her and remained forever engraved in her memory: Faced with the dangerous fire, the ants split up into pairs and two by two, side by side, pressed close together, they waited for death.

■

Brian Fawcett's *Cambodia: A Book For People Who Find Television Too Slow* also blurs fiction and essay. On the top of each page appear parables—some fantastic, others quasi-journalistic—all of which are concerned with media's colonization of North American life (both Fawcett and Coupland are Canadian). On the bottom of each page, meanwhile, runs a book-length footnote about the Cambodian war. The effect of the bifurcated page is to confront the reader with Fawcett's central motif: Wall-to-wall media represents as thorough a raid on individual memory as the Khmer Rouge.

■

In *U and I,* Nicholson Baker writes: "I wanted my first novel to be a veritable infarct of narrative cloggers; the trick being to feel your way through each clog by blowing it up until its obstructiveness finally revealed not blank mass but unlooked-for seepage-points of passage." This is a useful description not only of Baker's first novel, *The Mezzanine,* but of all of these books. Narrative progression is an apparent contradiction of literary collage, which compels instead by thematic orchestration, internal investigation, and the rubbing together of the author-narrator's emotional trouble with cultural cataclysm of some sort.

No wonder I'm such a fan of the form and of these books in particular: They're all madly in love with their own crises. In the following half a dozen collages, the crises vary, but in each case I try to wed my experience to a larger human perplexity and thereby go both further into myself and further away.

Downward

—⟋ℳ⟍—

THERE HAS ALWAYS been some strange connection for me between basketball and the dark. I started shooting hoops after school in third grade, and I remember dusk and macadam combining into the sensation that the world was dying but I was indestructible.

One afternoon I played HORSE with a second grader, Renée Hahn, who threw the ball over the fence and said, "I don't want to play with you anymore. You're too good. I'll bet one day you're going to be a San Francisco Warrior."

Renée had a way of moving her body like a boy but still like a girl, too, and that game of HORSE is one of the happiest memories of my childhood: dribbling around in the dark but knowing by instinct where the basket was; not being able to see Renée

but smelling her deodorant mixed with sweat; keeping close to
her voice, in which I could hear her love for me and my life as a
Warrior opening up into the night. I remember the sloped half-
court at the far end of the playground, its orange pole, orange
rim, and wooden green backboard, the chain net clanging in the
wind, the sand on the court, the overhanging eucalyptus trees,
the fence the ball bounced over into the street, and the bench the
girls sat on, watching, trying to look bored.

The first two weeks of summer Renée and I went steady, but
we broke up when I didn't risk rescuing her in a game of capture
the flag, so she wasn't around for my tenth birthday. I begged my
parents to let Ethan Saunders, Jim Morrow, Bradley Gamble,
and me shoot baskets by ourselves all night at the court across
the street. My mother and father reluctantly agreed, and my
father swung by every few hours to make sure we were safe and
to bring more Coke, more birthday cake, more candy.

Near midnight, Bradley and I were playing two-on-two
against Jim and Ethan. The moon was falling. We had a lot of
sugar in our blood, and all of us were totally zonked and totally
wired. With the score tied at eighteen in a game to twenty, I took
a very long shot from the deepest corner. Before the ball had
even left my hand, Bradley said, "Way to hit."

I was a good shooter because it was the only thing I ever did
and I did it all the time, but even for me such a shot was doubt-
ful. Still, Bradley knew and I knew and Jim and Ethan knew,
too, and we knew the way we knew our own names or the bat-
ting averages of the Giants' starting lineup or the lifelines in our
palms. I felt it in my legs and up my spine, which arched as I
fell back. My fingers tingled and my hand squeezed the night

in joyful follow-through. We knew the shot was perfect and when we heard the ball (a birthday present from my parents) whip through the net, we heard it as something we had already known for at least a second. What happened in that second during which we knew? Did the world stop? Did my soul ascend a couple of notches? What happens to ESP, to such keen eyesight? What did we have then, anyway, radar? When did we have to start working so hard to hear our own hearts?

Behold my agony as I contemplate the attempted apotheosis of NBA star Vince Carter. For if I join the hallelujah chorus concerning his "work ethic" and deference to his older teammates, his absence of jewelry and tattoos and showboating, his desire to "do things the right way," his postgame ritual of calling his mom and then playing video games rather than going to bars and clubs, his apparent contentment in Toronto, I feel as if I've been unwittingly enlisted in an anti-Allen Iverson, anti-Latrell Sprewell, neocon crusade in service of the old (supposed) verities—politeness, niceness, humility. Growing up in the Bay Area suburbs in the 1960s and '70s, I was instructed by my mother and father to write denunciatory editorials about the insufficiently desegregated school district; I was dragged into the city for civil rights and antiwar marches what seems in memory every third weekend. Given my background, I'm surprised and even a little embarrassed that, during the first and second rounds of last year's Eastern Conference playoffs, I rooted for Carter's Raptors against both Sprewell's Knicks and Iverson's Sixers.

As members of the Borel Junior High Bobcats, we worked out in
a tiny gym with loose buckets and slippery linoleum and butch-
er-paper posters exhorting us on. I remember late practices full of
wind sprints and tipping drills. One day the coach said, "Okay,
gang, let me show you how we're gonna run picks for Dave."

My friends ran around the court, passing, cutting, and screen-
ing for me. All for me. Set-plays for me to shoot from the top
of the circle or the left corner—my favorite spots. It felt as if the
whole world were weaving to protect me, then release me, and
the only thing I had to do was pop my jumper. Afterward, we
went to a little market down the street. I bought paper bags of
penny candy for everybody, to make sure they didn't think I was
going to get conceited.

In the series against New York, Carter won the final two games
for Toronto only after his own teammate prodded him to assume
his alpha role. In the series against Philadelphia, he was criticized
by his own coach for deciding to attend graduation ceremonies
in Chapel Hill the morning of the final game, which Toronto
lost. Still, it's hardly Carter's fault that his mother was a school-
teacher and his stepfather was a high school band director; that
after leaving the University of North Carolina a year early for the
NBA he—per the agreement he signed with his mother—took
correspondence courses in order to earn his degree in African-
American Studies; that, according to one childhood friend, "he
was raised to have morals, he was raised not to act better than

anyone else," and, according to another friend, "whenever I need advice, I call Vince. He's the best listener I know." What's so bad about being good? Isn't our collective romance with evil getting a bit boring in its own way? Why must Iago always get the best lines? Isn't it sweet (if a bit odd) that Carter's mother is proud he's regarded as a "mama's boy," that Carter's teammate Dell Curry says, "Vince is definitely the man I'd like to see my sons growing up to be," and that his former coach Butch Carter once complained, "He lacks a mean streak"?

■

The junior varsity played immediately after the varsity. At the end of the third quarter of the varsity game, all of us on the JV, wearing our good sweaters, good shoes, and only ties, would leave the gym to go change for our game. I loved leaving right when the varsity game was getting interesting; I loved everyone seeing us as a group, me belonging to that group, and everyone wishing us luck; I loved being part of the crowd and breaking away from the crowd to go play. And then when I was playing, I knew the crowd was there, but they slid into the distance like the overhead lights.

As a freshman I was the JV's designated shooter, our gunner whenever we faced a zone. Long-distance shooting was a way for me to perform the most immaculate feat in basketball, to stay outside where no one could hurt me. I'd hit four or five in a row, force the other team out of its zone, and then sit down. I wasn't a creator. I couldn't beat anyone off the dribble, but I could shoot. Give me a step, some space, and a screen—a lot to ask for—and I was money in the bank.

Throughout my freshman and sophomore years the JV coach told me I had to learn to take the ball to the basket and mix it up with the big guys underneath. I didn't want to because I knew I couldn't. I already feared I was a full step slow.

■

Images magnify the body. Television traffics exclusively in images. The NBA traffics, almost exclusively, in African-American bodies, and from the time the first slave ship pulled into the harbor, African-American bodies have been big sellers. "I propose," as Ralph Ellison says in *Shadow and Act,* "that we view the whole of American life as a drama acted out upon the body of a Negro giant." And now of course the drama is being acted out as well in Toronto and being exported around the globe. My friend, a 6'5" African-American businessman who worked for several months in Tokyo, said he spent a portion of nearly every lunch hour explaining to people that he wasn't a basketball player. When does history begin, in other words? When does it end? Is the NBA a sport, a business, or reparation theatre? To what extent are players interested in such questions? To what extent can one insist that players be interested in such questions? If you're not angry, are you just not paying attention? Are these my questions, or my parents' questions?

■

The next summer I played basketball. I don't mean I got in some games when I wasn't working at A&W or that I tried to play a couple of hours every afternoon. I mean the summer of 1972 I played basketball. Period. Nothing else. Nothing else even close to something else. All day long that summer, all summer, all night until at least ten.

The high school court was protected by a bank of ice plants and the walls of the school. Kelly green rims with chain nets were attached to half-moon boards that were kind only to real shooters. The court was on a grassy hill overlooking the street; when I envision Eden, I think of that court during that summer—shirts against skins, five-on-five, running the break till we keeled over.

Alone, I did drills outlined in an instructional book. A certain number of free throws and lay-ins from both sides and with each hand, hook shots, set shots from all over, turnaround jumpers, jumpers off the move and off the pass, tip-ins. Everything endlessly repeated. I wanted my shoulders to become as high-hung as Warriors star Nate Thurmond's, my wrists as taut, my glare as merciless. After a while I'd feel as if my head were the rim and my body the ball. I was trying to put my head completely inside my body. The basketball was shot by itself. At that point I'd call it quits, keeping the feeling.

My father would tell me, "Basketball isn't just shooting. You've got to learn the rest of the game." He set up garbage cans around the court that I had to shuffle-step through, then backpedal through, then dribble through with my right hand, left hand, between my legs, behind my back. On the dead run I had to throw the ball off a banked gutter so that it came back to me as a perfect pass for a layup—the rest of the game, or so I gathered.

Who am I, in other words, to tell Vince Carter how he should feel about his own life? What's *that* fantasy all about—the self-congratulatory yet masochistic liberal white dream about black men and their perpetual downness? Carter didn't grow up impoverished; on the contrary, he was raised in a 4,000-square-foot house in Daytona Beach. Nor has he publicly said he was ever the victim of any particularly overt racism. He's been treated as a deity since high school, when, beginning his junior year, scalpers gathered outside the gym two hours before his games.

■

The varsity coach was wiry and quick, and most of us believed him when he alluded to his days as a floor leader at Santa Clara. He never said much. He showed a tight smile, but every now and then he'd grab you by the jersey and stand you up against a locker. Then he'd go back to smiling again.

The first few games of my junior year I started at wing for the varsity. In the first quarter against a team from Redwood City, I got the ball at the top of the key, faked left, picked up a screen right, and penetrated the lane—a rarity for me. My defender stayed with me, and when I went up for my shot we were belly-to-belly. To go forward was an offensive foul and backward was onto my butt. I tried to corkscrew around him but wasn't agile enough to change position in midair. The Redwood City guy's hip caught mine and I turned 180 degrees, landing on my leg. My left thigh tickled my right ear. I shouted curses until I passed out from the pain.

I had a broken femur and spent the winter in traction in a hospital. My doctor misread the X-rays and removed the body cast too early, so I had an aluminum rod planted next to the bone, wore a leg brace, and swung crutches all year.

In the summer, the brace came off and my father tried to work with me to get back my wind and speed, but he gave up when it became obvious my heart wasn't in it. Senior year I was tenth man on a ten-man team and kept a game journal, which evolved into a sports column for the school paper. I soon realized I was better at describing basketball and analyzing it than playing it. I was pitiless on our mediocre team and the coach called me Ace, as in "ace reporter," since I certainly wasn't his star ballhawk. I could shoot when left open but couldn't guard anyone quick or shake someone who hounded me tough. I fell into the role of the guy with all the answers and explanations, the well-informed benchwarmer who knew how zones were supposed to work but had nothing to contribute on the floor himself. To my father's deep disappointment, I not only was not going to become a professional athlete; I was becoming, as he had been on and off throughout his life and always quite happily, a sportswriter.

■

Maybe the best thing to do, then, is just concentrate on Vince Carter the Basketball Player, specifically Vince Carter the Dunker, since that's why he's been anointed, in his own words, "the next 'man.'" A previous anointee, Grant Hill, has nothing especially spectacular about his game; there's nothing about his body begging to be fetishized. Carter, by contrast, has what Woody Allen once called "thrill capacity": George C. Scott is a great actor, but Marlon Brando rearranges our neurons. After Carter nearly single-handedly defeated the Lakers, Shaquille O'Neal called him "half a man, half amazing," and Kobe Bryant said, "Vince has got wings, man. I've seen him do stuff that's crazy." In a game a couple of years ago against Dallas, Carter took off from around the free-throw line, spun counterclockwise 360 degrees, carrying the ball in his right hand as a waiter would carry a tray; when he completed his turn, he put his left hand on the ball and jammed it through the hoop. Afterward, asked about this play, Dallas's Steve Nash said of Carter, "He's one of those guys who might do something you'll never see again."

That summer I went to the San Mateo County Fair with Renée Hahn, who had finally forgiven me for not rescuing her in capture the flag. Her knowledge of basketball hadn't increased greatly over the years, but she did know she wanted a pink panda hanging from a hook near the basketball toss.

The free-throw line was eighteen rather than fifteen feet away and the ball must have been pumped to double its pressure, hard as a bike tire. My shot had to be dead on or it would bounce way off. I wasn't going to get any soft rolls out of this carnival. The rim was rickety, bent upward, and was probably closer to ten feet, six inches than the regulation ten feet. A canopy overhung both sides of the rim, so I wasn't able to put any arc on my shot. With people elbowing me in back, I could hardly take a dribble to get in rhythm.

I won seven pandas. I got into a groove, and sometimes when I got into a groove from eighteen feet straightway, I couldn't come out of it. Standing among spilled paper cups and September heat and ice and screaming barkers and glass bottles and darts and bumper cars, Renée and I handed out panda bears to the next half dozen kids who walked by. This struck me then, as it does now, as pretty much the culmination of existence: doing something well and having someone admire it, then getting to give away prizes together. Renée wound up working with me on the high school paper the next year; I don't think I ever saw her happier than she was that afternoon.

■

ESPN The Magazine, naming Carter the "new millennium's athlete of the future," said, "We can't take our eyes off of him—in or out of uniform," and he "delivers the best three seconds in sports." (How long does an orgasm last, anyway?) I, too, have come not just to praise Carter but to hijack him for my purposes, only what exactly are those purposes? To rebel, mildly, against my parents' politics and to remind myself that even an ordinary person from the middle class might have something in him that's amazing.

■

I still like to roam new neighborhoods, tugging on twine, checking out the give. I like jumping up and down on concrete courts, feeling young again. In Cranston, Rhode Island, there's a metal ring that looks like hanging equipment for your worst enemy. In Amherst, Virginia, a huge washtub is nailed to a tree at the edge of a farm. Rims without nets, without backboards, without courts, with just gravel and grass underfoot. One basket in West Branch, Iowa, has a white net blowing in the breeze and an orange shooter's square on the half-moon board. Backboards are made from every possible material and tacked to anything that stands still in a storm. Rims are set at every height, at the most cockeyed angles, and draped with nets woven out of everything from wire to lingerie. From Port Jervis, New York, to Medford, Oregon, every type and shape of post, court, board, and hoop.

I once felt joy in being alive and I felt this mainly when I was playing basketball and I rarely if ever feel that joy anymore and it's my own damn fault and that's life. Too bad.

Properties of Language

My first name, "David," means "beloved" in Hebrew. My last name, "Shields," was originally "Schildkraut" until my father changed it after the war. My fate is inscribed in my name: Out of who knows what fear, I shield myself from my beloved. A more optimistic interpretation would, of course, see my name indicating that I shield my beloved, or that my beloved shields me, but part of the problem is that such glosses seem to me too glossy.

Immediately after entering the door, Gabriel Conroy humiliates Lily by offering her a coin for helping him off with his coat. Freddy Mullins is unable to complete the story he's telling because he erupts in bronchitic laughter. Although none of the "Three Graces" have been paying attention to Gabriel's speech, they're overcome with emotion at its pathos. Shortly before he leaves Misses Morkan's Annual Dance, Gabriel tells a story about a man who gets furious at his horse when the beast, out of habit, walks round and round a statue rather than proceeding to the destination, a military review. Gabriel recalls poignant moments that he and his wife, Gretta, have shared, but the last scene he remembers is her asking a man making bottles in a roaring furnace if the fire is hot. At the very moment Gabriel is trembling with desire for her, in a rented hotel room, Gretta remembers Michael Furey, her childhood sweetheart, and breaks loose from her husband. Desire never transmutes into fulfillment; dissonance never resolves into harmony. Throughout the Christmas party, throughout "The Dead" and all of *Dubliners,* throughout pretty much the last hundred years of literature, conversations are interrupted, subjects are dropped, songs suddenly break off, physical movements are jerky and abrupt. Something in the voice catches.

■

Benna Carpenter, the protagonist of Lorrie Moore's novel *Anagrams,* says, "There is only one valid theme in literature: Life will disappoint you." Love, in *Anagrams,* is never not seen against the background of death, never not seen in the context of physiology, evolution, devolution. Benna thinks about some birds: "From four blocks away I could see that the flock had a kind of group-life, a recognizable intelligence; no doubt in its random flutters there were patterns, but alone any one of those black birds would not have known what was up. Alone, as people live, they would crash their heads against walls."

Where's the fun here? Where it always is: in the words. Or, more precisely, in the pleasure as well as the terror Benna derives from the mutable nature of language. "I've always been drawn to people who misspeak," she says. "I consider it a sign of hidden depths, like pregnancy or alcoholism." (When I first read *Anagrams,* I developed a crush on Lorrie Moore, as do so many other male writers; her punning and acidity make her seem like some fantasy sparring partner for the language- and irony-besotted. She gave a reading at her alma mater, where I was then teaching, and I hoped, a little naively, that she'd find my speech impediment irresistible.) *Anagrams* is suffused with varieties of misspeaking, and the central passage of the book, the last argument Benna has with her ex-husband, is organized around her mishearing "I never want to see you again" as "I want to see you again."

Benna's realization that "sloppiness was generally built into the language" tarnishes for her every act of communication, but it also causes her to conjure up pillow talk with Georgianne, her make-believe daughter: "'Do you want to?' she [Georgianne] squeaks, in imitation of someone, something, I don't know what, and she tweaks my nose, my skinny merink, my bony pumpkin." Pure love is pure language. Feeling becomes sound.

■

My blood pressure zoomed to 150/100. Rachel suggested that I try Transcendental Meditation. She'd abandoned it long ago, after only a few months, but it had helped her stop smoking

so much pot. At my TM initiation ceremony, I was informed
that "Sho-ring" was my mantra. After a few days, I told my TM
teacher I couldn't use "Sho-ring" because every time I said it
aloud all it signified to me was how to perform a marriage pro-
posal. I asked for another mantra. The teacher said no.

The summer between my freshman and sophomore years of college, I worked at the Rhode Island Historical Society, where I
transcribed—in chronological order—the letters of a Revolutionary War general who occasionally would write home and
tell his wife how much he loved her. These letters, in which he
pledged his fidelity and tried to evoke her beauty with a few col-
orful adjectives, were discussed reverentially by the old women I
worked with in the fourth-floor transcription room. There was
something formal and predictable in his tone that rang false to
me and in general I didn't believe the general, but I suppose his
wife tried to and the widows and spinsters I worked with tried
even harder. It was a tough day at the Society when we all read the
letter in which he wrote back to her after she'd written to him and
tried to explain why she was marrying the children's tutor.

In *Reading Stanley Elkin,* Peter Bailey discusses Elkin's novella
"The Making of Ashenden," in which the protagonist beds a
bear: "In choosing the language of sensuality and anti-social impulse over the lure of romantic self-annihilation, Ashenden frees
himself into possibility, tempering his taste with the awareness
of the bestial in himself and expanding his notions of heritage to

include among the air, earth, water, and fire one additional element—honey." This is perfect-pitch sit-down comedy, told with
a straight face and in the shaping straitjacket of formal exegesis.
Conveying Brewster Ashenden's WASP gravity, Bailey creates
high humor—T.S. Eliot testing the sound system at the Improv.
Stanley Elkin was sort of a St. Louis St. Jude, patron saint of lost
causes. Himself a victim of multiple sclerosis, Elkin's *dramatis
personae* includes an anhedonic bully, a doomed wanderer, a talk
show host out-talked by his audience, a man sent to hell, a man
without history. Rather than dispelling the usual objections to
Elkin's work—its episodic verbosity, its shtick—Bailey absorbs
them into his own argument for the unique excitement of Elkin's fiction: the sheer sound of his words, the elaboration of his
metaphors. As is the case with most Elkin novels, Bailey's book
doesn't really go from Point A to Point B let alone Point C; instead, it just keeps circling down, getting deeper, darker, fuller of
a complex sorrow whose only consolation is the spunky speech
borne of that sorrow.

A student in my class, feeling self-conscious about being much
older than the other students, told me that he had been in prison.
I asked him what crime he had committed, and he said, "Shot
a dude." He wrote a series of very good but very stoic stories
about prison life, and when I asked him why the stories were so
tight-lipped, he explained to me the jailhouse concept of "doing
your own time," which means that when you're a prisoner you're
expected not to burden the other prisoners by complaining about
your incarceration or regretting what you had done or, especially,

claiming you hadn't done it. "Do your own time"—it's a seductive slogan. I find that I quote it to myself frequently, but really I don't subscribe to the sentiment. We're not, after all, in prison—not exactly, not literally. Stoicism bores me. What I ultimately believe in is talking about everything until you're blue in the face.

One of my clearest, happiest memories is of myself at fourteen, sitting up in bed, being handed a large glass of warm buttermilk by my mother because I had a sore throat, and she saying how jealous she was that I was reading *The Catcher in the Rye* for the first time. As have so many other unpopular, oversensitive American teenagers over the last fifty years, I memorized the crucial passages of the novel and carried it around with me wherever I went. The following year, my older sister said that *Catcher* was good, very good in its own way, but that it was really time to move on now to *Nine Stories,* so I did. My identification with Seymour in "A Perfect Day for Bananafish" was extreme enough that my mother scheduled a few sessions for me with a psychologist-friend of hers, and "For Esmé—with Love and Squalor" remains one of my favorite stories. In college, I judged every potential girlfriend according to how well she measured up to Franny in *Franny and Zooey.* In graduate school, under the influence of *Raise High the Roofbeam, Carpenters* and *Seymour, An Introduction,* I got so comma-, italics-, and parenthesis-happy one semester that my pages bore less resemblance to prose fiction than to a sort of newfangled Morse code.

When I can't sleep, I get up and pull a book off the shelf. There are fewer than ten writers whom I can reliably turn to in this situation, and Salinger is one of them. I've read each of his books at least a dozen times. What is it in his work that offers such solace at 3 AM of the soul? For me, it's how his voice, to a different degree and in a different way in every book, talks back to itself, how it listens to itself talking, comments upon what it hears, and keeps talking. This self-awareness, this self-reflexiveness is the pleasure and burden of being conscious, and the gift of his work—what makes me less lonely and makes life more livable—lies in its revelation that this isn't a deformation in how I think; this is how human beings think.

Before she knew me, Rachel worked one summer as a graphic artist in a T-shirt shop in Juneau, Alaska. Cruise ships would dock, unloading decrepit old passengers, who would take taxis or buses a dozen or so miles to Mendenhall Glacier, which is a hundred square kilometers—25,000 acres—and whose highest point rises a hundred feet above Mendenhall Lake. A tourist once said about the glacier, "It looks so dirty. Don't they ever wash it?" On their way back to the boat, one or two of them would invariably come into the shop and ask Rachel if she'd mail their postcards for them. Able to replicate people's handwriting exactly, she would add postscripts to the postcards written by the ancient mariners: "Got laid in Ketchikan," "Gave head in Sitka," etc.

What do I love so much about this story? I could say, as I'm supposed to say, "It's just so Rachel" or "I don't know, it just makes me laugh," but really I do know. It's an ode on my favorite idea: Language is all we have to connect us, and it doesn't, not quite.

S & M: A Brief History

—ɯ—

I HAD BEEN awake for a while, playing music low, walking around the room hanging up clothes. I lifted up the covers, pinched Rachel's ass, and whispered, "Got change?"

I never had change. I hated to break a dollar, but I also hated to be late for work. With all the walking around the room I did, I could have walked up and back to work twice.

"Close the curtains," Rachel said.

I sat down on the edge of the bed and said, "I need bus fare."

Her jeans were in a heap on the floor. I turned the pants pockets inside out, spilling coins on the rug.

"Don't just take my money," she said.

"What am I supposed to do, make a formal—"

"Flip a coin," she said. "Double or nothing."

"What do you mean?" I've never been much of a gambler.

"Money, suck my toes; no money, no toesucking."

I said, "I'm late."

"Flip a coin," she said. "Call it."

"Tails."

Rachel sat up in bed, caught the coin in midair, pushed on the back of my head until my lips were nuzzling her feet, and said, "You win."

■

In *Pain & Passion*, the psychiatrist Robert Stoller presents his thesis regarding the origin of "sadomasochistic scripts. The major traumas and frustrations of early life are reproduced in the fantasies and behaviors that make up adult eroticism, but the story now ends happily. This time, we win. In other words, the adult behavior contains the early trauma. The two fit: The details of the adult script tell what happened to the child."

In the first of the eight interlocked stories or chapters of *Butterfly Stories: A Novel,* William Vollmann tells "what happened to the child," establishing the psychic interconnection— for the butterfly boy—between solitude, beauty, loss, pain, and punishment. The lyric catalogue of childhood humiliations in the first story yields, in the following seven stories, to litanies of the butterfly boy (who as an adult is called first "the journalist," then later "the husband") re-enacting—with a lesbian traveling companion, the son of a former SS officer, a sybaritic and amoral photographer, and especially with a Phnom Penh prostitute named Oy—the sadomasochistic scenarios of his childhood.

"I don't know why I like to sleep so much," Rachel liked to say. "I guess because it's so easy."

She got lost in bathrooms. She felt safe in them, at home, locked in. She had a toilet kit like a suitcase. She liked to be clean. She talked about towels and soaps and different kinds of tissues (their warmth, their softness). She liked to play with faucets and shower curtains and swinging mirrors. Transfixed on beauty, Rachel stared into mirrors for hours, scaring away blemishes.

Vollmann begins *Butterfly Stories* with the evocation of war torture by the Khmer Rouge: "Sometimes they peeled away their skins and ate their livers while the victims were still screaming. Sometimes they wrapped up their heads in wet towels and slowly suffocated them. Sometimes they chopped them into pieces." On the next page, he writes: "There was a jungle, and there was murder by torture, but the butterfly boy did not know about it. But he knew the school bully, who beat him up every day." Vollmann thus makes absolutely explicit the link between the butterfly boy's childhood and his adult experiences in Thailand and Cambodia.

The eponymous butterfly boy "was not popular in the second grade because he knew how to spell 'bacteria' in the spelling bee, and so the other boys beat him up. Also, he liked girls. Boys are supposed to hate girls in second grade, but he never did, so the other boys despised him. Very quickly, the butterfly boy realized that there was nothing he could do to defend himself. To every other boy in the school, the butterfly boy was so low and vile that he was not a human being. So the butterfly boy's pleasures were of a solitary kind. One evening a huge monarch butterfly landed on the top step of his house and he watched it for an hour. It squatted on the welcome mat, moving its gorgeous wings slowly. It seemed very happy. Then it rose into the air and he never saw it again. He remembered that butterfly for the rest of his life." The butterfly boy thinks about the school bully: "The substance that his soul was composed of was pain," but this is at least as true of the butterfly boy.

■

The most attractive quality in the world to me was Rachel's unrepentant superficiality. I thought she had things to teach me; she did, but not the things I thought. I would recognize her voice anywhere—its inexpressibly erotic faux neutrality. I was happy captive to her expertly delineated imitations of indifference, which, for all I know, weren't even especially imitations.

■

The relationship between "the journalist" and the prostitute Oy, which forms the central thread of *Butterfly Stories,* is reminiscent, for me, of *The Good Woman of Bangkok,* Dennis O'Rourke's autobiographical documentary film about journeying to Thailand and falling in love with a Thai prostitute. Vollmann is much more rigorous than O'Rourke, though, more painstakingly and painfully honest. He has a merciless eye for the economies of desire: "A middle-aged midget in a double-breasted suit came down the alley, walked under one girl's dress, reached up to pull it over him like a roof, and began to suck. The girl stood looking at nothing. When the midget was finished, he slid her panties back up and spat onto the sidewalk. Then he reached into his wallet."

■

Rachel was appalled by the place I was subletting on Greenwich Avenue, so she rented us a room at the Washington Square Hotel. Chocolate brown walls, paisley bedspread. A guy behind Plexiglas let us into the building each time with a buzzer. I was leaving the next day, so we stayed up all night and had nothing to say to each other. She kept going out and coming back with another little bag of cookies from David's Cookies, which produced the most touching tableau: Rachel lying on her stomach on the paisley bedspread, licking the dripping David's chocolate off her clothes and hands, while I licked her from behind. It was as if I were licking shit through her, then out her, out her mouth, onto the shitty walls.

■

In our last argument, Rachel said, "Get the fuck out of my apartment, you fucking asshole. What the fuck do I care?" Like dialogue in a snuff film. Like a parody of our harmful relationship. Like a line lifted from our next-door neighbor's less reflective life. Cliché of cliché, fact of facts: It made me hard. "You're a ghost," she said. "You're yesterday. You're already memory, sweetheart."

Rhetorical questions: Why are women drawn toward men wearing uniforms? "Where were you," shrieked the bum, spitting against the driver's-side window of the black BMW stopped at a light at Fifth Avenue and Fourteenth Street, "when I was in Vietnam?" Why do balloons make adults depressed? *Why,* asked the bill of Rachel's favorite cap, *are you reading my cap?* Why do I miss Rachel so much?

Butterfly Stories is told in more than two hundred very short sections. In the last quarter of the novel, Vollmann appends to the conclusion of several sections the words "The End," as if to suggest the ceaselessness of the butterfly boy's capacity for self-inflicted punishment. After acting out "endless" scenarios of humiliation and loss, "the husband," who may have AIDS, returns in the final chapter to San Francisco, self-consciously trying—and failing—to play his spousal role: "Sometimes he'd see [his wife] in the back yard gardening, the puppy frisking between her legs, and she'd seem so adorable there behind window-glass that he ached, but as soon as she came in, whether she shouted at him or tried desperately to please him, he could not feel. *He could not feel!*"

Butterfly Stories is built upon the following irony: In this extraordinarily intimate book about the butterfly boy's incapacity for ordinary intimacy, I—as reader—couldn't get any closer to the butterfly boy if I crawled inside his skin.

A hotel room in Manzanillo, Mexico. For recreation, Rachel lay, like a virgin sacrifice, across the white kitchen counter and said that the only fantasy she'd ever had was to open her legs as wide as she could and, under virtually gynecological scrutiny, be admired. Just that. So female. Be admired. She leaned back. Her bikini bottoms flapped about her ankles. I got into position.

Possible Postcards from Rachel, Abroad

—ɯ—

The Greek word "eros" denotes "want," "lack," "desire for that which is missing." The lover wants what he does not have. It is by definition impossible for him to have what he wants if, as soon as it is had, it is no longer wanting. This is more than wordplay.

—Anne Carson

Hi, David. Here I am in Geneva. The Swiss have the second-largest standing army in the world. They can mobilize their entire force in less than 30 minutes. All men 18 and older serve one week per year in the army, running drills and practicing shooting (I'm sure you'd love that!), or doing paperwork when they get older (more your style). They all have loaded rifles and pistols at home in their closets. I guess they want peace at any cost. They made me wait in a crowded room for my physical exam just to be allowed into the country. I had my chest X-rayed for tuberculosis. Sitting there, I realized that everyone around me was from somewhere else: Senegal, Lebanon, Turkey. I feel like the only one of my kind here. I feel like the outsider.

I'm sitting on the Quai Wilson during the Fêtes de Genève (the annual carnival). To my left is a group of young women fully dressed in Arabic clothing (sharia and jilbab). One of them thinks I don't see that she's staring at my naked skin—bare legs, bare feet, bare arms, neck, hair being free. I assume that she's hot under her black robe and that she wishes she could be as free to choose as I am. It's only when they turn to leave and our eyes meet that I realize what I see on her face is not envy but pity. I miss talking to you about stuff like this.

Went out with my friends last night in Geneva. We went dancing at L'usine. "Black Night" or "Nuit Black," as my young friends call it. (Do you feel old now, too?) Most of them are from Senegal and Ethiopia and know nothing about PC. They celebrate their differences in language and culture, and they know that here the Arabs and the Portuguese are "below" them (in the Swiss's opinion). "At least we speak French" is what they say. I didn't realize the Swiss hated anyone openly. I'm learning a lot. I feel colorless with them. It's nice.

On the bus on my way to work today in downtown Geneva, I saw a group of banner-carrying Serbs smash the glass bus shelter right in front of the U.N. They were burning the grass into a word I didn't recognize. Our bus driver took one look at them and lowered the arm to the electric cable, taking an alternate route. When I came

back after work, the only sign of it ever having taken place was
that the grass had been mowed to a new, short length and the burnt
parts sprayed with what I guess was some sort of Astroturf paint.
There was nothing on the news that night. If a word is written, and
no one reads it, does the word exist? Is this the sort of esoterica
you're still interested in?

Got strip-searched in Tel Aviv while trying to leave the country. I'm
sure it seemed suspicious—two young Americans, holders of U.N.
travel cards, coming to Israel for a four-day vacation. But that's
what it was. My friend Matthew took me on a crazy four-day vacation before his move to Hungary. They examined our bags first,
X-rayed my shoes, and ripped the film out of my camera, before
making me stand in my underwear while the inspector checked me
out. (Jealous?) I guess being white and female doesn't always mean
you're above suspicion. Matthew thinks it's his fault: He's sure they
could tell he's gay.

I'm in the Zurich train station, waiting for the train to Berlin. Next to
me is a large family—Romanian? Hungarian?—with trash bags and
battered suitcases. Their whole lives are jammed into these bulging
cases. When they begin speaking, I lean in to hear what they're saying. It's yet another language I don't speak. When will I know enough
languages? When will I be more than just an American woman?

■

Matthew's boyfriend Nicholas wants me to marry him. No, it's not quite like it sounds. He's French and holds a Swiss C-permit (next best to being a citizen) and I, of course, have the almighty green card behind me. It's tempting to imagine offering my future children all of these passports—all of these opportunities. Knowing me and my great guilt, it probably won't happen. And besides, Matthew would kill me. Um, why didn't you and I ever get married? Because being with each other we scared ourselves. (Nearly wrote "scarred," which is true, too.)

■

Things the Merrill Lynch lawyer told me about Swiss work-permit renewals: 1) I can stay for two separate periods of three months after it expires (with 24 hours somewhere else in between). For this I'll need to go to the *contrôle des habitants* with *annonce de départ* and get a *visa touristique.* 2) I can stay as a student and work 20–25 hours a week. I'd need to get a new permit. 3) I can try to get a job with the U.N. (I won't need any permit to work for them). The lawyer hates this idea—of course, he's Swiss. 4) If I marry a Swiss or a person with a C-permit, I will get a C-permit immediately. This is illegal. Guess I'll apply to the U.N.

■

Not one but three offers: The first is with the International Organization for Migration, the second with the World Intellectual Properties, and the third with the World Health Organization. I think I'm going to take the IOM job. I'll be working with a team of people creating a database and statistical reports that track immigration and refugee movements. If I stay long enough, I could get sent to

work at one of the missions—Africa, Hungary, Thailand, Haiti. I'll
actually be having an effect on people's lives. I'm sure this seems
hopelessly idealistic to you, but the world is a real place, *monsieur.*

■

I found out today that the man I rent a room from goes to Thailand
twice a year and sleeps with Thai prostitutes. While cleaning the
living room, I found some photographs of beautiful young Thai girls
and I asked him about them. He told me that if he weren't sleeping with them, someone else would be and that at least he was dis-
ease free, nonviolent, and generous with his tips and gifts. I had
heard that this sort of thing happened, but I never knew anyone
who actually did it. He's not bad looking—he's a dead ringer for that
guy (Patrick?) we used to go to movies with in LA—and he's young
enough and interesting enough to get a woman over here, or so I
thought. He said that the girls are young, sometimes virgins, and
that they always ask him to marry them. Well, no kidding, I said.
He's Swiss and, in their eyes, he offers them a freedom they've never
known. He says he's even considering it. They don't even speak his
language. I think he just wants a sex slave. (Now, if he only wanted
to *be* a sex slave . . .) He's really highly ranked in the Swiss army
and—get this—his name is *Christian.* Perfect. Time to look for a new
apartment.

■

Went to L'escalade and watched people run through the windy
streets in the cold. The race is run every year to symbolize the
retreat of the Duke of Savoie's army. They run through Geneva's
steep streets and climb its many flights of stairs. Matthew bought

me a marmite (a chocolate cauldron filled with brightly colored
marzipan vegetables). It's a symbol of the Mère Royaume housewife
who killed an invader with a hot cauldron of vegetable soup when
the Duke of Savoie was trying to take over Geneva. She defeated
him and the city remained free. Europeans turn all of their attacks
and wars into holidays.

I love the winter holiday season in Geneva. Mont Blanc and Le Salève
(local mountain) are white-capped and the air is crisp and cold. The
city is decorated in old-timey lights and ribbons, and everywhere I
go are vendors selling roasted chestnuts. I wait for the tram, holding the warm cone of nuts in my hands, smelling their richness, and
watching the Swiss. They stroll past, hand-in-hand, red-cheeked and
smiling. I don't know how, but they remain sweetly childlike in their
fascination with holidays. *Très* kitsch, but I am chock-full of longing
and envy; I'm sure you can relate.

Szia! See ya! That's how you say the Hungarian word for hello.
I've been in Budapest, visiting Matthew for a few days now, and I
couldn't understand why everyone was telling me goodbye right
when I first met them. Our word for goodbye is theirs for hello.
This place feels so steeped in history and yet so modern. Young
Hungarian women wear such short shorts that there's not much
left to the imagination (even your overheated one). They mostly
have great bodies and they dress as if they're waiting to be discov-
ered by *Vogue*. And yet they all live at home; families of 10 or more
people share 3 rooms. It's hard to reconcile the fact that Hungary
was shuttled back and forth between the Germans and the Russians

with the fact that Hungarians remain such gentle and open people. It only makes sense when I see that all of the Communist stars—on bridges, buildings, statues—haven't been removed, merely covered with a thick canvas. Nothing is permanent.

In Budapest, foreigners must carry Hungarian money on them at all times. If the police stop you and you can't show them the money, they kick you out of the country. This is their solution to "squatters." Last week a friend of mine got caught and thrown in jail. After he'd gotten back to Romania, I didn't hear from him for a week. He'll sneak back in later next week; he needs to find a job to support his family. I told him I'd give him some money to carry in his pockets. He said that it wouldn't help; he's a *tzigane* (gypsy) and looks like a *tzigane* and will always be forced to leave: See ya!

Driving through northern Italy with friends. The beauty of this area amazes me. Mountains and water—so green and blue that only Italian could describe them. And the black gray of the tanks that appear quickly as we move through the switchbacks. Europe never lets you forget that you are fragile, that you are different from everyone else on the planet, that this difference is both lovely and awful. Ah, but you already knew this, we knew this together, didn't we, sweetheart?

Love, Rachel

On Views and Viewing

—ᴍ—

I WAS STANDING in Victory Video in a godforsaken village in northern New York—too far north to even be called "upstate" New York. The girl behind the counter was wearing an usher's outfit and munching popcorn. Victory Video carried (by mistake, I think) Henry Jaglom's *Always,* which I adore, so I got it and the girl behind the counter asked to see my driver's license. She commented upon how happily few numbers my California driver's license had, compared to New York's, then said, "I wouldn'ta left California for nuthin'." Which had the quality somehow of an accusation: I had been living in Xanadu and left; what could possibly be the matter with me? It was a good question, and she looked into my eyes for the answer.

■

"Don't hate me because I'm beautiful."

"It only works if you watch."

"It's only live once; don't miss it."

"You're at a stoplight. It will last thirty seconds. This may be the only time some people ever see you. How do you want to be remembered?"

"You never get a second chance to make a first impression."

"And isn't that a nice reflection on you?"

■

Rachel maintained and periodically updated what she liked to call her "little black book," which consisted exclusively of two kinds of entries: feature articles concerning performing artists whose work she admired, and pictures of summer houses she yearned to occupy. I must admit I found myself riffling through the pages of this album for unconscionably long periods of time: I couldn't shake the feeling that it functioned somehow as a sort of talisman to disarm bearers of bad news.

■

"Aw . . . shit . . . I hate this . . . I hate this fucking life," the blind man said, startling everybody. "Fuck you, God."

■

"For all of us who try to make sense of a world that sometimes doesn't . . ."

"In a world of constant change, there's one certainty."

"Mr. Goodbar—a simple pleasure in a complex world."

"I wish the rest of my life were as simple."

"Ours is not a perfect world, but Diet Coke may be the perfect thirst-quencher."

"In a world where time stops for no one, you can stop it and hold it with a Polaroid Spectra System."

Several years ago my friend Doron saw an ad for "free housing" on an estate on Fishers Island in exchange for "light groundskeeping." He applied and won the job over many applicants, because he could be convincing that he was handy with tools. The "housing" turned out to be a large, dreary garage apartment, on a run-down estate. The new owners were in their early thirties, with five young kids. The estate had a huge, shaggy lawn, neglected fruit trees, a garden infested with rabbit warrens, and a trout pond whose resident eels ate all the trout as soon as they were stocked. The agreement was that Doron would cut the huge lawn each week with a lawn tractor, and with whatever hours were left over after that, would do gardening and handy work— up to sixteen hours a week. He would have to work only during the summer months, when the family was in residence. During the winter they lived in Manhattan; Doron would get the house, paying only for utilities.

He found it took almost twelve hours to cut the lawn, but he also fixed a dock and a garden gate, planted a big garden. At the owners' insistence, he pruned the fruit trees after they'd already begun to leaf. The owners wildly complimented his first efforts and began smilingly asking him to do this and that. Once, he

was called into the main house to fit a loose hinge on a cabinet
door. He could tell by the gouges in the wood that the owners
couldn't figure out which way a wood screw turned out. (I say
this as if I know which way a wood screw turns out or even precisely what a wood screw is; I don't; this is just the way Doron
told me the story.) They put pressure on him to do more and
more. He resisted, citing the original agreement. Eventually the
owners and he had a screaming fight, and he quit. He lasted out
the winter by fishing for food.

Before things turned sour, though, he enjoyed the making
of the family portrait. The owners had hired a famous portrait
painter much admired by the rich of Manhattan. He could
paint you representationally, but heroically *moderne*. He took a
huge photo of the family all posed outside the house on Fishers
Island. He agreed to paint in for a background a wild point of
land reaching into the turbulent waters of Long Island Sound.
This was a place where he and others surf-fished on the island at
dusk, but where summer people never dared tread at any time
of day. It was near the end of the small airstrip on the island
where several light planes bringing in the gentry for weekends
had recently, and fatally, crashed in the fog.

The artist went back to New York City for a month and
painted in the bodies as posed in the photo. Then he came
back to the island to do the faces. He did one at a time, posing
the person as his or her body had already been painted in, on
the grass of the lawn of the shabby estate. But all the subjects
were restless. They had no contemplative skills. They couldn't
hold themselves still for more than several minutes. The painter
finally fixed on the strategy of running an extension cord out of

the garage and plugging in a portable TV set just to the side of the painter. The subjects would watch TV and the painter would paint the faces.

■

Even when a window looks out onto water, I usually pull the shade. I've never been a big fan of a view.

■

Interfrequency broadcasters.
Video fishtanks.
Waxed produce.
Talking tombstones.
Talking vending machines.
The fluorescent lights at McDonald's.
McNugget Buddies shaped like Chicken McNuggets.
Drive-in funeral parlors.
People meters.
Visual telephones.
Nursery monitors.
Speaker packs.
Telegrams demanding that we burn their contents.

■

I recently went by myself to ring the doorbell of my childhood home in the Griffith Park section of Los Angeles. No one answered, so I looked around a little outside. The brick wall was gone, the garage was replaced by a deck out back, and the living room appeared to have been turned into a wet bar. Incense burned out open windows. What was once a white and lower-middle class neighborhood was now integrated and middle class. I could remember only a few things about the house in which I lived the first six years of my life: between the front lawn and the front porch, the brick wall which served as an ideal backstop for whiffleball games; an extraordinarily cozy living room couch on which I would lie and watch *Lassie* and apply a heating pad to relieve my thunderous earaches; the red record player in my sister's room; and the wooden rocking horse in mine . . .

I'd hold the strap attached to his ears and mouth, lifting myself onto the leather saddle. One glass eye shone out of the right side of his head; its mouth, once bright-red and smiling, had chipped away to an unpainted pout. His nose, too, was bruised, with gashes for nostrils. He had a brown mane which, extending from the crown of his head nearly to his waist, was made up of my grandmother's discarded wigs glued to the wood. Wrapping the reins around my fist, I'd slip my feet into the stirrups that hung from his waist. I'd bounce up and down to set the runner skidding across the floor. Then I'd sit up, lean forward, press my lips to the back of his neck, and exhort him. (Infantile, naive, I thought I could talk to wooden animals.) I'd wrap my arms around his neck and kick my legs back and forth in the stir-rups. I'd lay my cheek against the side of his head, press myself to his curves. When he pitched forward, I'd scoot up toward the base of his spine, and when he swung back I'd let go of his leather strap and lean back as far as I could, so I was causing his motions at the same time as I was trying to get in rhythm with them. I'd clutch him, make him lurch crazily toward the far wall, jerking my body forward, squeezing my knees into wood. Then

I'd twist my hips and bounce until it felt warm up under me, bump up against the smooth surface of the seat until my whole body tingled. I'd buck back and forth until it hurt, in a way, and I could ride no longer. Who would have guessed? My very first memory is of myself, in my own room, surrounded by sunlight, trying to get off.

■

In Kafka's story "First Sorrow," the trapeze artist wants only to live up on the trapeze his entire life. Then he has his first sorrow: He wants to add a second trapeze bar (he's getting lonely up there all by himself).

■

"I believe in Crystal Light because I believe in me."
"For the most important person in my life: me."
"To be what we are, to become what we are capable of becoming, is the only end of life."
"How you can find happiness during the collapse of civilization . . ."

■

Bob Hope referred to one show business legend after another until David Letterman got so exasperated he asked, "Don't you know any normal people?" Bob Hope said, "Normal people?" Asked what his goal in life is, Letterman said, "To be remembered as not just another show biz asshole." He once asked an actress, whose name even Rachel could never remember, if a single thing she'd said tonight was true. The actress said no. And yet what keeps me coming back is not just his contempt for the artificial—he's Holden Caulfield; he hates phoniness—but the way, as the camera pulls back, he'll lean over and whisper only to guests he likes; the way, the moment the mike's off, he'll disconnect it, remove his coat, and pointedly shun his last guest (whoever it is), as if to suggest he literally can't wait to return to his real life, whatever that might be.

■

"We were watching a rerun of *The Brady Bunch* and my cousin Mike, who works at ComputerWare, pointed out something pretty relevant to my situation: Greg Brady is way too old to still be in high school." These were the first words of a monologue spoken to me many years ago in an Amtrak dining car. The rest of the monologue went about like this: "He looked okay in the real early ones when they all had crew cuts, but then they kept him in high school for eight more years. It's like Richie Cunningham. I mean, how many years can you be in eleventh grade? The point Mike was making was they secretly have these older people play teenagers just to make us feel like totally inadequate shits. Even in a show like *James at 16,* which later became *James at 17,* they got this guy Lance Kerwin to play James. Not that he was bad at it, mind you. But when I compared myself with this guy, it didn't seem right. Okay, here's an example. There's this Swedish exchange student. Inga's her name. In real life, she's the girl who does the ads for Flex hair conditioners. The girl with the cowboy hat and the gun. The one who married Joe Montana. Well, James helps her with her English and shows her around town. Evidently Inga really appreciates what he does for her, because when James gets all romantic, puts on Billy Joel's

The Stranger, and whispers all this mushy shit to her, she lets him fuck her silly on the couch. How am I supposed to react to this? Say, 'Way to go, James; next time let me meet her sister'? It's like I'm just supposed to sit in my room and wait for some girl with big tits to come down from outer space like E.T. and enter my life . . .

"Mike stayed at this party and I walked around the town for a while. There was this bar with a sign that read 'Nude Dancing Nightly—Luscious Ladies.' So I went in to see if I could catch some action. The place was pretty seedy. Lots of weird old men sitting at these big long tables, but no luscious lady dancers anywhere in sight. I asked the bouncer about the lack of dancing nude women and he just said, 'No dancing tonight. Tomorrow.'

"Understandably disappointed, I sat down at the end of the bar and ordered myself the most important-sounding drink I could think of. *Brian's Song,* my favorite movie of all time, was playing on the TV. Even in a bar, it was a very touching experience. In fact, I can honestly say that by the end of the movie, there wasn't one person in the whole place that didn't have one of those sore lumps in the bottom of his throat . . .

"I shaved my head and joined this cult that fucks sheep. Ha ha, only kidding. There was this movie where all these people actually do that, though. It was on Cinemax last month. I can't think. Not just today, every day. I used to go the mall, but since Christmas shopping started, everybody wants to know what time it is and slush gets all over your shoes . . .

"Everything has become so much better since we got cable. Used to be that nothing was on after *The Flying Nun.* But now with WTBS the Superstation, you can watch *Hazel, Bewitched,* and *Perry Mason* all right in a row. Too bad that Della Street got charged with murder on this new movie they made. It was pretty good, but the guy who played Paul Drake wasn't the same. He was his son or something. From what I understand, they might make a sequel . . .

"Mike has this theory that explains why you never see girls half as good-looking in real life as the girls in the videos on MTV. Mike's idea is that there's this island, sort of like Fantasy Island, where all the beautiful girls on MTV live. They are real live Amazon women who kill lions with spears and stuff. That's why they're so hot and sexy; they eat raw flesh and it turns them on."

■

"Coke is it."

"Cherry 7-Up: Isn't it cool in pink?"

"We do it like you'd do it when we do it at Burger King."

"It's better in the Bahamas."

"The It girl."

"Do it now."

"Just do it."

"You're soaking in it."

■

"I'm a receptionist at a travel agency," my friend Stephanie wrote to me. "We all wear uniforms. We are stewardesses not yet in the air."

■

Rachel asked me, "Why do you always say, 'I hate this guy, I hate that guy'?"

"Like who?" I said. We were in the car on the way to a movie. The radio was on.

"Oh, I don't know. Tom Cruise. X. Y."

"Courtney Love. Z. That guy on channel four."

"Exactly," she said.

"I don't know," I said, although of course I did know. Both of us knew. We all know. We resent that we're members of a religion with such flimsy gods.

■

"Now this . . ."

"Fourteen: fourteen after the hour."

"Something will be happening today, and you should be the first to know about it."

"Give us eighteen minutes and we'll give you the world."

"Remember: We're in touch, so you be in touch."

■

The student lecture board distributed flyers announcing a lecture by the then-famous R., and at the bottom of each flyer was the statement, in bold letters dwarfing the rest of the announcement, "This event was scheduled on extremely short notice to allow CBS to film it." We all went.

The Problem of Distance

—⁓—

In Nicholson Baker's novel *The Fermata,* Arnold Stine develops the "power to drop into the Fold. A Fold-drop is a period of time of variable length during which I am alive and ambulatory and thinking and looking, while the rest of the world is stopped, or paused . . . All the laws of physics still obtain, as far as I can tell, but only to the extent that I reawaken them. The best way to describe it is that right now, because I have snapped my fingers, every event everywhere is in a state of gel-like suspension . . . It's a sort of reverse Midas touch that I have while in the Fold—the world is inert and statuesque until I touch it and make it live ordinarily."

■

The protagonist of Kathryn Harrison's novel *Exposure*, Ann
Rogers, is the thirty-three-year-old daughter of Edgar Rogers,
whose photographs are scheduled to appear in a retrospective
at the Museum of Modern Art. The photographs document
Ann, as a child, in various poses of "self-mutilation and sexual
play . . . Edgar Rogers's fame depended on his daughter: Every
photograph of note was of Ann. Cautious, he stuck with a successful theme—Ann posed as if dead—and over the years, as
she grew and changed, there was something increasingly fascinating and seductive in the fact that it was the same child, the
same girl, teenager, woman, who died a thousand deaths for the
camera." When the retrospective of her father's work is moved
up from the fall to the summer in response to demonstrators
protesting "work of an offensive and misogynistic nature," Ann
reverts to her habit of shoplifting in Manhattan's most exclusive
stores. Walking around Bergdorf Goodman, planning and ex-
ecuting her latest heist, she's clearly drawn toward, even aroused
by, the presence of hidden cameras and undercover detectives.
Only what is hidden, what is secret, has the frisson for her of remembered (even if dangerous and painful, especially if dangerous and painful) experience. Harrison frequently interpolates
into the text excerpts from newspaper articles, Ann's father's
letters, museum catalogues, court proceedings, contracts, tele-
phone answering-machine messages. It's as if Ann can charac-
terize herself only as a series of documents in her father's never-
ending documentary.

In my book *Remote*, I write, "When I was a little kid, I was a very good baseball player, but I actually preferred to go over to the park across from our house, sit atop the hill, and watch Little Leaguers, kids my age or younger, play for hours. 'What's the matter with you?' my father would ask me. 'You should be out there playing. You shouldn't be watching.' I don't know what's the matter with me—why I'm adept only at distance, why I feel so remote from things, why life feels like a rumor—but my father was right: Playing has always struck me as a fantastically unfulfilling activity."

In Daniel Richler's first novel, *Kicking Tomorrow,* set in Montreal in the mid-1970s, Robbie Bookbinder, the eighteen-year-old leader of the punk band Hells Yells, likes a stripper named Rosie and loves a heroin addict named Ivy, and "here are some drugs he figured a person can handle in moderation: Mary Jane, obviously, kif, too, honey oil, all that. Bennies of any variety (blackbirds, cartwheels, cranks, dexies, greenies, jelly babies, lid-poppers, pink amps, green amps, crystal meth, you name it). What else—snappers, gunk, stinkweed. All the kitchen conveniences: catnip, mellow yellow, wild lettuce, kola nuts, nutmeg, parsley, fennel, dill. And the stuff in the cabinet: paregoric and Valium and Demerol. What else?" The change Richler rings on the coming-of-age genre is that Robbie isn't so much an angry or sensitive as an exceedingly bored young man, a rebel wannabe with a million excuses. "It's all my fault," his mother, a talk show host and environmental activist, says about the fact that their family is holding Seder in September. "I was just too busy in the spring." "I've always wondered," Robbie asks his grandmother, "and since I don't speak Hebrew, what exactly *coleslaw* means." Robbie's a nice Jewish boy who wants to but can't quite embody (because for one, he can't quite remember) the Surrealist slogan to which Ivy subscribes: "Beauty will be convulsive, or not at all."

■

Many of what seem to me the most illuminating books and movies about American media-culture—Brian Fawcett's *Cambodia: A Book for People Who Find Television Too Slow,* Marshall McLuhan's *Understanding Media,* William Gibson's *Neuromancer,* Douglas Coupland's *Generation X,* David Cronenberg's *Videodrome,* Atom Egoyan's *Family Viewing*— come from Canada. In *Him with His Foot in His Mouth,* Saul Bellow, who was born in a Montreal suburb, says, "Canada's chief entertainment—it has no choice—is to watch (from a gorgeous setting) what happens in our country [America]. The disaster is that there is no other show. Night after night they sit in darkness and watch us on the lighted screen."

■

Frenesi Gates, the heroine of Thomas Pynchon's novel *Vineland,* once belonged to "24fps, the old guerilla movie outfit"; she once wanted to "wrap each day, one by one, before she lost the light"; the other members of 24fps were trying to decide whether they were willing to "die for shadows."

■

In Janette Turner Hospital's novel *The Last Magician*, Lucy, the narrator, asks Charlie, an avant-garde photographer, why he takes photographs so "constantly, so obsessively, why he collects *other* people's photographs, why he scavenges in secondhand shops and buys, by the shoe-box full, old, cracked, brown-and-cream records of other people's pasts."

"So that I will see what I've seen," he says.

■

The ostensible subject of Frederick Barthelme's novel *The Brothers* is sibling rivalry. Its true subject is Del Tribute's attempt to reclaim his presence in the world by seeing it as breathtaking, as beautiful. In the opening paragraph, "it'd quit raining, and the sunlight was glittery as he crossed the bridge over the bay, but his fellow travelers didn't seem to notice the light." Later, Del says, "There isn't any story. It's not the story. It's just this breathtaking world, that's the point. It's like the story's not important—what's important is the way the world looks. That's what makes you feel the stuff. That's what puts you there." When Del and his girlfriend are at the Singing River Mall, "Del thought it was beautiful. 'Nobody really gets this,' he said. 'Nobody sees how gorgeous this is or knows why.'" Del says about storms that "they transform everything instantly. It's like suddenly you're in a different world and the junk of your life slides away and you're left with this rapture, this swoon of well-being and rightness. You get the world in its amazing balance." By the end of the book, "it was one of those nights when the air is like a glove exactly the shape of your body."

VI.

YOU AS ME

Other People

—⁂—

"OKAY, OKAY, OKAY, we get it: You stutter and so, irredeemably self-conscious, you're devoted to yourself as a subject, also as a symbolic subject, even as some sort of featured player in a collage movie. Don't you finally want to get outside yourself? Isn't that finally what this has to be about, getting beyond the blah-blahblah of your endless—" Yes, yes, a thousand times yes. Or, rather, yes and no. I want to get past myself, of course I do, but the only way I know how to do this is to ride along on my own nerve endings; the only way out is deeper in; the only portraits I'm really interested in are self-portraits as well. I'm just trying to be honest here.

I'm drawn to writers who appear to have Heisenberg's Uncertainty Principle tattooed across their foreheads: The perceiver by his very presence changes the nature of what's being perceived. In the afterword to *Lolita*, Nabokov mentions "a newspaper story about an ape in the Jardin des Plantes, who, after months of coaxing by a scientist, produced the first drawing ever charcoaled by an animal: This sketch showed the bars of the poor creature's cage." I admire Hilton Als's *The Women*, W.G. Sebald's *The Emigrants*, and V.S. Naipaul's *A Way in the World*—books in which the chapters, considered singly, are relatively straightforwardly biographical, but read as a whole and tilted at just the right angle, refract brilliant, harsh light back upon the author. I admire Geoff Dyer's book about D.H. Lawrence, Nicholson Baker's about John Updike, and Nabokov's about Gogol, in which one author tries to write about another author but, trapped in the loop-the-loops of his own consciousness, winds up writing a self-portrait that is also, obliquely, a parable about the ostensible subject (the other author). "I only know an object in so far as I know myself and my own determination through it," Hegel says, "for whatever I am is also an object of my consciousness, and I am not just this, that or the other, but only what I *know* myself to be. I know my object, and I know myself; the two are inseparable."

In the following four chapters, the arrows are meant to be pointing in both directions: outward toward other people and inward toward my own head. What we have here is a failure to communicate, but not entirely. I just want to foreground that failure and, by foregrounding it, get past it out into the world.

Are You Who I Think I Am?

—⁊⁊⁊—

Human kind
Cannot bear very much reality.

—T.S. Eliot

SCOFFED THE MOTHER whose beautiful baby girl had just been praised: "You should see her pictures."

"Hey: twins!" someone said as the father pushed his daughters down the street in a stroller. "Like the movie."

"You're good, doll," the Mafioso inamorata said in the video store commercial, "but Palmer Video's better."

When asked whom, in her entire life, her favorite lover was, Greta Garbo said, "The camera."

"If I don't have a tan," the actor said, "I feel naked."

Said the Ford dealer with a certain mild but unmistakable exasperation over the phone, "It's a color not found in nature."

"If this isn't interesting," said the talk show host about beauty contestants getting plastic surgery, "I don't know what is."

Explained the fashion designer, "I want to make every man feel as perfect as he aspires to be."

"*Things* rule and are young," the marketing director explained. "*Things* confront and replace one another."

"Boldness is part of the marketing strategy," the marketing executive said, "because Doritos is already perceived as kind of a bold product."

"If you don't recognize that song," said the oldies DJ, "that's because it's new."

"Anyone this self-contained," the movie reviewer observed about the movie star, "must know something important."

"Don't ever change anything," the casting director advised his newest find, "except your underwear."

"I don't like the term 'extras,' because you're all individuals," the casting director said on another occasion, dividing people into rows of body types. "I'd rather call you 'background artists.'"

"Actor Paul Newman's daughter Susan is coming to Potsdam," the weekly shopper informed us, "as part of her crusade against the glamorization of drug and alcohol abuse in the media."

Halfway through the hour-long interview, the rock star explained to the interviewer, "We don't do interviews."

"I'm psyched," said the passenger as the plane reached a cruising altitude of thirty-one thousand feet. "I've got *People*."

Asked to name the elements he looks for in a headline, the editor of the tabloid newspaper replied, "Sex. Violence. Money. Children. Animals."

When an actor, appearing on a talk show, claimed that everyone was watching the new game show he was hosting, the talk show host said, "Oh, really—everyone? Is Saul Bellows?"

"Have I," the writer was asked, "read anything you've written?"

The country music star said, "We salute the Country Music Association for doing its part to improve reading skills among children with a series of television commercials."

"How many of you *physically* went to see the movie *Six Pack*?" asked the country music star turned movie actor. "I got paid on the basis of how many people went to see it, and I can't believe they're all here."

"I make my own movies," said the camcorder enthusiast, "just like real life."

"I can't believe I saw him," the woman from Phoenix said about the Pope. "I got a picture of him looking right at the lens. I can't wait to see it developed. I had tears coming through the lens."

"Radio is like the Old Testament—hearing wisdom, without seeing," the televangelist explained. "Television is like the New Testament, because in it the wisdom becomes flesh and dwells among us."

"Bernadette Peters is in it," said the theatergoer, urging her friend to attend the play with her. "She's beautiful. She came from TV."

"I realize I should take a day off, go to the beach, fall in love or something," the television executive acknowledged, "because you have to experience things so you can think, 'Wouldn't that be nice to get on television.'"

"If you don't have anyone," the sexy young television actress told a nationwide audience on Valentine's Day, "I'll be your valentine." (Sad to say, her condescension, her narcissism made me, briefly, miss Rachel more.)

"This is wonderful," the photographer told the model, "it's like you're making love to the camera," to which the model replied, "That's exactly what I do. I put someone I love inside the camera and remember them looking at me. I see their face."

"Thank you," the comedian said to his audience at the end of his set. "You were delightful."

"Are you," asked the fan of the television interviewer, pausing, making sure to get the words right, "who I think I am?"

"When I'm looking at you," wrote the soap fan to the soap star, "are you looking at me?"

Encountering the familiar face of a fading star but unable to place her, the fan asked, "Who did you used to be?"

"Hello, Frank Gifford," said the sportscaster at the top of the show. "I'm everybody."

"I'm not even going to try to explain my emotions," said the newly unemployed college football coach to the cameramen and reporters. "You guys, if a guy was in a car, drowning, you'd stick that damn mike through the only space left in the window."

"If you want to know more," we were told at the end of the hour-long documentary about stress featuring Bobby Knight, Martin Sheen, and Joan Rivers, "here are some books you can read . . ."

Explained the heavily perspiring man who agreed to have his quadruple bypass filmed, "There's no way they're going to lose me on live TV."

"Carlos Montalban, 87," the obituary read in its entirety, "the man known to millions as the picky coffee-bean buyer El Exigente in the Savarin commercials; of a heart ailment, in New York City, March 28."

The travel agent explained, "You can't call up and say, 'My brother died; can I have his World Perk miles?' He has to will them to you."

"Sorry to hear that," the play-by-play man said after being informed on the air that a former colleague of his had died. "Back at the Oakland Coliseum . . ."

"It renders everyday events rather meaningless," the sportscaster said about a player's death, "but here are tournament scores from around the country . . ."

"When the first child went down," the teacher said about one of the six second graders shot by the madwoman, "my first thought was, 'They're filming a movie and they forget to tell me. They just forgot to tell me.'"

"We went to a funeral before going to see *There's Something About Mary*," the member of the audience testified to the people shooting the commercial, "and it really cheered us up."

"Many thanks for your recent article," the Cemetery Association wrote to thank the reporter for his feature on pilgrimages to Bruce Lee's grave. "Just the right amount of restrained pizzazz we like to see."

"With the dead," explained the postmortem photographer, "you don't have to worry about exposure time."

Asked to define "solitary confinement," the prison warden said, "No television. No magazines. No radio. No newspapers. No movies."

Doubt

—〰—

ADAM SANDLER IS widely perceived to be a dolt, a mascot for low mediocrity rewarded. I don't know about his movies. I haven't seen any of them with the exception of *The Wedding Singer*, whose silliness = sweetness I rather liked. I have, though, listened to "The Chanukah Song" about a hundred times; it gets at Jewish ambivalence about Jewishness, at my ambivalence about Jewishness (about simultaneously wanting to be a part of the moronic goyische culture surrounding us and wanting to be apart from it), as acutely as anything I know.

Virtually every cut from Sandler's CD *What the Hell Happened to Me?*—even the title mimics Jewish angst—is a barely disguised ode to dispossessed people, animals, and things, such as a chained goat, a piece-of-shit car, a neurasthenic Southerner, a senile grandmother. Sandler begins "The Chanukah Song" by telling a live audience of college students that there are many Christmas songs but not very many Chanukah songs (Jewish apology for being Jewish in a Christian culture). So, Sandler informs us, he wrote a song for all the nice little Jewish kids who don't get to hear any Chanukah songs. This is Jew as victim, Jew as "nice." Is it important to Sandler to create a little distance between himself and nice little Jewish kids? Is it important to me to do the same? If so, why?

In the first stanza, Sandler says that Chanukah, a festival of lights, is coming and is fun, so everybody should put on their yarmulkes. Repetitively strumming an electric guitar, unable to carry a tune, he sings these lines with good-Jewish-boy poignance, sweetness, yearning. ("The Chanukah Song Part II," on another CD, doesn't work for me at all. The balance between feeling and mockery which Sandler maintains so delicately in the first version tips over completely into parody in the later version and is therefore, given my emotional geography—bound by ambivalence—off the map.) He undermines the whispery solemnity, though, when he says "eight crazy nights" with a self-conscious, Steve Martinesque craziness. Chanukah isn't about "crazy nights"; neither is Judaism; neither am I. The song is going to make the case that Jews are capable of Dionysian craziness, and what makes the song so appealing to me is that even as Sandler makes this assertion, he also winks about it, knowing it's not especially true. I can count on one hand the number of times I've ever been drunk or high. Okay, two hands.

In the second stanza, Sandler says that Kirk Douglas, James

Caan, Dinah Shore, and David Lee Roth are Jewish "just like you and me." Sandler sings these lines with ostensible self-pity, which he—again—undercuts by laying way too much schmaltz on "just like you and me." This list of people who are Jewish is, of course, a send-up of Jewish head-counting, of "what's good for the Jews," and yet it's also genuine boast. Sandler is a creature of popular culture, so it's natural for him to name celebrities, but to me—only to me, because I look like, or at least strive to look like, an absent-minded egghead urban intellectual?—it's heartbreaking that none of the four people he mentions "look Jewish," and they all are, or were, sex symbols, based more or less on their Aryan good looks. *Here are people we're proud of,* Sandler seems to be saying, *but we're proud of them because they look like you*—the audience of college kids at the University of California at Santa Barbara to whom he's singing and blonder than whom there doesn't exist. The audience goes wild, clapping in rhythm. *We love you for being Jewish, Adam,* I seem to hear them saying, *Jewish just like us (blonde beauties).*

The third stanza does pretty much the same thing, with Paul Newman and Goldie Hawn—both half-Jewish—the new blonde, blue-eyed gods. "Put them together, what a fine-lookin' Jew," Sandler says sardonically, lampooning the sentiment at the same time that the upbeat music screams celebration. The next stanza gives us Captain Kirk and Mister Spock: "both Jewish," Sandler says in old-Jewish-man voice, mixing stereotype with anti-stereotype, as does the entire song. I remember how loudly my father laughed, sitting in the bathtub and reading *Portnoy's Complaint* the summer it was published, but how he couldn't help but wish only Jews would be allowed to read it, since it reified so many stereotypes.

In the fifth stanza he head-counts Rod Carew, Harrison Ford, Ann Landers, and Dear Abby, and outs former Seattle SuperSonics owner, Barry Ackerley (I've long wondered whether he's Jewish; is it only in Seattle that his Jewishness would be such a closely guarded secret?). The audience cheers wildly when Sandler informs them that O.J. isn't Jewish; the performance was recorded only a few weeks after the verdict. As O.J. is the anti-Jew (uncerebral to the point of being out of control; can I say that?), Rod Carew is the anti-O.J.—one of the greatest hitters in baseball history, whose success depended at least as much upon his mental agility as his physical prowess. No surprise about Ann Landers and Dear Abby—advice-giving yentas. Harrison Ford—the unJewish quarter-Jew. Sandler is riven by the same ambivalence that I am: Affirm Dear Abby (Mom) or Harrison Ford (not-Dad)?

In the next stanza we learn that the Three Stooges were Jewish and some people think Ebenezer Scrooge is; "Well he's not," Sandler says with transparent and, thereby, oddly moving defensiveness. *We're tired of fighting that image of ourselves; we're about the joyful lunacy of the Stooges, not the miserliness of Scrooge.* This upbeat message immediately gets rather fully contradicted, of course, as it must, since we're Jewish. Some consolation: Tom Cruise isn't Jewish, but his agent is. The stereotype—moneygrubber—is true?

In the final stanza, Sandler deepens the paradox by refusing to resolve it, combining "harmonicah," "gin and tonicah," "marijuanakah," and "Chanukah." This constitutes very modest wordplay, to be certain, but it's crucial, because through the repetition he's ridiculing his—my, our—need to Chanukahize everything, to declare that we're Jewish in a season when no one wants to be. At the same time that Sandler's pretending to affirm Jewish capacity for what I think he knows and what I know I know are unJewish Dionysian pastimes—getting drunk, getting high, getting crazy—what he's really affirming are his (my) own self-consciousness, cleverness, involution, ambivalence, pride, shame: Jewishness.

The Only Solution to the
Soul is the Senses

—⧙—

A FEW YEARS ago Bill Murray said in a radio interview: "I was one of the first people to really devote my entire life to the Weather Channel, which is what I do. I love the Weather Channel. The charm and the power of the fronts, you know. You get to see something really important happening. And it's dealt with in a really . . . there's even more talk about it, but nothing can be done." I'm in a swoon over Murray because he takes "my issues"—gloom, rage, self-consciousness, world-weariness—and offers ways out, solutions of sorts, all of which amount to a delicate embrace of the real, a fragile lyricism of the unfolding moment. He thus flatters me that under all my protective layers of irony I, too, might have depth of feeling as well. I admire his slouching insouciance but don't possess it, admire it precisely because I don't possess it. I realize, of course, that a certain redemptive posture is the unique property of movies and movie stars, but Murray's grace is manifest at least as often outside movies as in them. The first line of his book, *Cinderella Story: My Life in Golf,* is, "The light seems to come from everywhere."

In the last decade there have been a few exceptions—primarily *Groundhog Day* and *Rushmore*—but Murray has been so good in so many bad movies that it's as if he makes bad movies on purpose as a way to demonstrate the truth of Denis Leary's dictum (to which I subscribe), "Life sucks; get a fuckin' helmet." Murray's movies, in general, suck; he's the fuckin' helmet. In a self-interview in which he asked himself to explain why so few of his films have succeeded, he replied, mock-solemnly, "I've had lots of good premises." *The Razor's Edge* being, again, an interesting exception, Murray seems to believe that, given the horror-show of the universe, the supreme act of bad faith would be to appear in a pretentious work of art aspiring to be beautiful, whereas my impulse has always been to try to find in art my only refuge from the storm.

Murray's metaphor for the Sisyphean struggle is: "In life, you never have to completely quit. There's some futile paddling toward some shore of relief, and that's what gets people through. Only the really lucky get a tailwind that takes them to the shore. So many get the headwind that they fight and, then, tip over and drown." Life is futile; failure is a sign of grace; Murray is fuck-up as existential fool. His loserdom is the exact opposite, though, of, say, Woody Allen's, who seems intolerably sniffly by comparison. I'm much, much more like Allen than I am like Murray, which is why I admire Murray (Jewish adoration of unJewish stoicism). Asked to name people he finds funny, Murray mentions Bob Hope, David Letterman, Conan O'Brien, Eddie Izzard—WASPy wise-guys, goyischer slackers, no whiners allowed.

In *Meatballs,* Murray is counselor at a summer camp for losers. When they're getting demolished in a basketball game against a much tonier camp, Murray instructs his charges to run around pantsing their opponents. Forget the score; fuck the rules; do fun things; give yourselves things to remember. Camp director Morty takes himself and the camp way too seriously (so many blocking figures in Murray movies are officious Jews; what's that about—Hollywood's knee-jerk self-hatred?) and so Murray leads all the other kids in always calling him "Mickey," turning him into a mouse. The great crime in any Bill Murray movie is self-seriousness, because as Murray's fellow Irishman Oscar Wilde said, "Life is too important to take seriously." Wilde also said, "The only solution to the soul is the senses," which is a key to Murray's appeal: He's in touch with his animal self and teaches the kids to be in touch with theirs. We're all meatballs; we're all just bodies. If I were a girl or gay, I'd have a searing crush on him in this movie, because just the way he carries his body seems to say *Here is fun. I'm where fun happens.* When he (crucially: unsuccessfully) courts another counselor, he does so without an ounce of earnestness. Losers are winners; they get that life is an unmitigated disaster. At one point he leads the campers in a chant, "It just doesn't matter, it just doesn't matter, it just doesn't matter." My problem is that even though I know on an intellectual level that "it just doesn't matter," on a daily level I treat

everything like it does. Murray is notorious for and proud of the
degree to which he makes up his own lines in movies; I suppose
I could look up whether "It just doesn't matter" is in the original
screenplay of *Meatballs,* but I'd rather not. I want to believe it's
his invention.

Murray's shtick—anti-star Star, anti-hero Hero, ordinary-guy
Icon—is built in part upon the fact of his unglamorous appear-
ance. In sketches on *Saturday Night Live,* Gilda Radner would
often call him "Pizza Face," and it's obvious he's never done anything to improve his deeply mottled skin. Seemingly half my
adolescence was spent in a dermatologist's office. *Saturday Night
Live* producer Lorne Michaels said about Murray, "He never had
much vanity. There was a way he always told the truth." The
qualities are of course intricately intertwined; it's his absence of
vanity that allows him to get to emotional truths in a scene, as
opposed to, say, Tom Cruise, whom you can tell is always only
concentrating on one question: How do I look? I was cute enough
as a little kid to appear in an advertisement for a toy store; my
father took the photographs, and here I am in the family album,
riding a plastic pony and brandishing a pistol with crypto-cow-
boy charm. Although now I'm certainly not handsome, I don't
think I've ever quite outgrown that early narcissism. Murray's
not fat, but he has a serious paunch; as opposed to some middle-
aged buffster like Harrison Ford, Murray's fifty and looks all of
it. Bless him for that: It's a gift back to us; he makes us all feel
less shitty. He posed for a *New York Times Magazine* profile wearing a drooping undershirt and with uncombed, thinning, gray
hair. It's a comparison Murray would surely loathe for its la-di-
da-ness, but the photograph reminds me of Rembrandt's late

self-portraits: a famous man who understands his own mortal ordinariness and is willing to show you the irredeemable sadness of his eyes in which that knowledge registers.

Murray's sadness is not other movie stars' pseudo-seriousness; he seems genuinely forlorn—always a plus in my book. Speaking to Teri Gross on "Fresh Air," Murray said, "Movies don't usually show the failure of relationships; they want to give the audience a final, happy resolution. In *Rushmore,* I play a guy who's aware that his life is not working, but he's still holding on, hoping something will happen, and that's what's most interesting." Gross, stunned that Murray would identify so strongly with someone as bitter and remorseful as Herman Blume, tried to pull Murray up off the floor by saying, "I mean, you've found work that is meaningful for you, though, haven't you?" Murray explained that Blume is drawn to the energetic teenager Max Fischer, who is the founder and president of virtually every club at Rushmore Academy, but "sometimes it makes you sadder to see someone that's really happy, really engaged in life when you have detached." He said this as if he knew exactly what he was talking about. "Murray's glazed expression sees no cause for hope in the world," the film critic Anthony Lane once said of him. Nothing can be done. In *Quick Change,* co-directed by Murray, he plays a clown named Grimm. "What kind of clown are you?" he's asked. "The cryin'-on-the-inside-kind, I guess," he says, which—maybe it's me—I take both as goof on the cliché and true confession.

The Razor's Edge, co-written by Murray, is the only completely serious film he's ever done, the film which he had desperately been wanting to do for years and which the studio agreed to finance only after Murray first agreed to do *Ghostbusters II.* It's Murray's ur-story. The first part of the Maugham novel is set in Chicago, but Murray moved the first part of the film to Lake Forest, next door to Wilmette, the North Shore suburb in which he grew up. The bulk of the book and film are set in Paris, where Murray spent a year, studying French and Gurdjieff and fleeing from post-*Ghostbusters* fame. Surrounded by cripples and sybarites, amoralists and materialists, Murray's character in *The Razor's Edge,* Larry Durrell, travels to China, Burma, and India searching for meaning, and the best he can come up with is: "You don't get it. It doesn't matter." It just doesn't matter. Such is the highest wisdom a Murray character can hope to achieve: a sort of semi-Zen detachment, which only deepens his dread (sounds familiar to me).

Angst translates easily to anger. Wes Anderson, explaining why he'd been somewhat anxious about directing Murray in *Rushmore,* said, "I'd heard about him throwing someone in a lake on one thing, and I'd heard that if he didn't like the situation he's going to change it." Discussing megalomaniacal celebrities, Murray said, "Whenever I hear someone say, 'My fans,' I go right for the shotgun." In *Kingpin,* Murray plays an impossibly arrogant bowler who, in one scene, says hello to the two women sitting at the next table. The less attractive woman responds by saying, "Hi," and Murray says, "Not you [nodding to the less attractive woman]. You [nodding to the more attractive woman]." Murray explained to Teri Gross how he had ad-libbed the line: "It just came into my mind at that moment. And it was so horrible—such a horrible thing to say that there was a moment of complete disbelief and then everyone [on the set] laughed really hard because, you know, the guy should be taken out and shot. It was just the kind of thing that I think would be the most offensive thing you could do. I was trying to paint a picture of a guy who was really, really a bad guy, so that any second that Woody [Harrelson]'s character stayed with this guy was an investment in bad time." Murray can access his own cruelty but isn't defined by it. He simply doesn't radiate malevolence, as, say, James Woods used to do, but neither is he cuddlesome-cute, à la Tom Hanks; this mixture keeps me productively off-balance, makes me unsure whether to embrace him or be slightly afraid of him. I strive for the same mystery in my own persona but fail miserably, since it's so evident how much neediness trumps coolness. When Murray gave his protesting-too-much explanation to Teri Gross, she responded, "I guess I've always wondered how you so intuitively seem to understand a certain type of really crude, ego-driven personality." With genuine hostility in his voice, Murray said, "Well, that's a loaded question, Teri." Then he quickly downshifted back to a more mild tone—again, that nervous-making mixture: "But how do I understand that? I don't know. I think show business can enrich that. You can see people manifesting in a bizarre way that, you know, other people don't try to get away, wouldn't try to get away, with. But people get lost in a vanity space and just start going. You know, people that just take themselves too seriously—it's ripe for re-creation."

He seizes the regenerative power of behaving badly, being disrespectful toward condescending assholes, telling truth, as they say, to power. In his self-interview, in which he pretended to be discoursing with Santa Claus, he said, "I was at the New York Film Critics Circle Awards one year. They called me up

when somebody canceled two days before the thing, and asked
me to present some awards. So I went, and one of the funni-
est film moments I've ever had was when they introduced the
New York film critics. They all stood up; *motley* isn't the word
for that group. Everybody had some sort of vision problem,
some sort of damage. I had to bury myself in my napkin. As
they kept going, it just got funnier and funnier looking. By the
time they were all up, it was like, 'You have been selected as
the people who have been poisoned; you were the unfortunate
people who were not in the control group that didn't receive
the medication.'" This is a little amazing, even shocking to me;
I fancy myself something of a literary troublemaker, but I can't
imagine being quite this publicly dismissive toward the powers-
that-be in the book world (privately, I'm acid etched in acid, of
course—what bravery). I suppose his career is less dependent
than mine is upon good reviews, i.e., he's actually popular. "If
you're not angry, you're not paying attention," goes my favorite
bumper sticker. Murray's edginess is a product of the fact that
he actually pays attention. He has what Hemingway said was
the "most essential gift for a good writer: a built-in, shock-proof
shit detector."

Hemingway's hometown of Oak Park is about twenty miles
southwest of Murray's hometown of Wilmette; both men have
or had a gimlet-eyed view of the disguises the world wears. It's
more broadly Midwestern, though, than only Hemingwayesque,
I think. Dave Eggers, who grew up in Lake Forest, has it. Johnny
Carson, who was raised in Nebraska, and David Letterman,
who was raised in Indiana, also have it—this quality of detachment which is a way of not getting sucked in by all the shit sent

your way, of holding onto some tiny piece of yourself which is immune to publicity, of wearing indifference as a mask.

He is, in other words, ironic. He's alert to and mortified by the distance between how things appear to be and how they are. On *Charlie Rose*, the unctuous host kept trying to get Murray to brag; in every instance, Murray deflected the praise, lightly mocking himself (his irony is bottomless but never particularly self-lacerating). In *Polyester*, Murray sings "The Best Thing," a love song; it's telling, I think, that John Waters cast Murray to sing the parody–love song in the parody–love movie. In *Michael Jordan to the Max*, a grotesquely worshipful IMAX film-paean, Murray, as a fan in the stands, says, "It's like out of all the 50,000 top athletes since, you know, prehistoric times—brontosaurus and pterodactyls included—he [Jordan]'s right there." These are modest examples, but they betray Murray's impulse: to unhype the hype, to replace force-fed feeling with something less triumphal, more plausible and human and humble. In *Stripes*, Murray delivers a rousing speech to his fellow soldiers to encourage them to learn overnight what they haven't learned during all of boot camp—how to march. "We're Americans," he says, "we're all dog faces, but we have within us something American that knows how to do this." Murray saves the speech from sentimentality by mocking the sentimentality. *I'm not really in this situation,* Murray's character seems to be thinking; *I'm not really in this movie,* Murray seems to be thinking. That reminds us or at least me of our own detachment and puts us in the scene, thereby making the moment credible and, ironically, moving. Here, as in so many other Murray movies, Murray somehow manages to install a level or two of Plexiglas between himself and the rest of the movie. "What's funny about Murray is not his performance," the film critic Tom Keogh has written, "but the way he hangs back from his performance." At its most dire, Murray's persona is simply anti-feeling; at its most fierce it's anti-faux feeling. This is what gives his persona such an edge: It's unclear whether his self-mockery is saving grace or Nowhere Man melancholia. It's both, obviously, to which I can attest or hope to attest. Maybe detachment is a way to get to real feeling; maybe it's a dead end from which no feeling arises. That's the Murray bargain.

Murray's characteristic manner of delivering dialogue is to add invisible, ironic quotes around nearly every word he says, as if he weren't quite convinced he should go along with the program that is the script, as if he were just trying out the dialogue on himself first rather than really saying it to someone else in a movie that millions of people are going to see, as if he were still seeing how it sounds. The effect is to undermine every assertion at the moment it's asserted. As a stutterer and writer, I'm a sucker for Murray's push-pull relationship to language; it's undoubtedly one of the main sources of the deep psychic identification I've always felt toward him. Commenting upon Murray's performance as Polonius in the most recent film adaptation of *Hamlet,* the film critic Elvis Mitchell said that Murray's Polonius is "a weary, middle-aged man whose every utterance sounds like a homily he should believe in and perhaps did many years ago." Murray simultaneously embodies and empties out cliché, showing how much we don't believe it, how badly we want to. In *Tootsie,* as Dustin Hoffman's roommate who's a playwright/waiter, Murray says about his work-in-progress, "I think it's going to change theatre as we know it." Murray says the line in a way that no one else could: We're aware that he's full of shit, but we're also aware that he's aware he's full of shit. For which we adore him, because he reminds us how full of shit we are every hour of every day. He's also a welcome relief from Dustin Hoffman's earnestness.

His pet technique for underlining his self-consciousness is knocking, loudly, on the fourth wall. Serving as guest broadcaster for a Chicago Cubs baseball game, which Murray once said is the best thing he's ever done, he answered the phone in the adjoining booth, stuck out his tongue at the camera, called down to the players on the field. On the first episode of the *David Letterman Show,* Murray ran into the audience and led them in an insanely spirited rendition of Olivia Newton-John's "Let's Get Physical." In *Stripes,* when his girlfriend leaves him, he turns to the camera and says, "And then the depression set in." At pro-am tournaments, Murray wears goofy outfits, jokes with the crowd, hits wacky shots—in an effort to tear a hole in the sanctimonious veil surrounding the game of golf. In *Michael Jordan to the Max,* Murray shoves his tub of popcorn at the camera and asks, "Hey, can I ask you: How big does that look on IMAX? Does that look like a gigantic bucket of popcorn or not that big?" At a Carnegie Hall benefit concert with a Sinatra theme, Murray, backed by a full orchestra, sang "My Way"; Murray told an interviewer, "I basically rewrote the lyrics and changed them around to suit my own mood. I started getting laughs with it, and then I was off the click track. I mean, there's a full orchestra playing to its own charts, so they just keep playing, you know. And the fact I'm off the lyric and talking and doing things—it doesn't matter to them. They don't keep vamping; it's not like a piano bar. They just keep going to the end. So I said let's see if this big band is going to stay with me here, and they didn't. They just kept barreling right ahead. But I managed to catch them at the pass. I headed them off at the pass and turned it around and got out of it again." It's crucial to Murray's comedy that the orchestra is there, playing away, serious as society—the formal straitjacket he wriggles out of. By far my favorite joke I've heard recently goes:

> Knock-knock.
> Who's there?
> Interrupting Cow.
> Interrupt—
> Moo.

Murray and I—other people, too, obviously—share an impulse to simultaneously annihilate and resuscitate received forms. I have an extraordinarily vivid memory of a very brief video clip I saw twenty years ago of a juggler who was riding a unicycle and pretending to have great difficulty controlling the knives he was juggling. He was in absolute control, of course, but I loved how much trouble he pretended to be having; I loved how afraid he pretended to be; I loved how much it was both a parody of the form and a supreme demonstration of the form. I loved it so much (an artist pretending death was going to win, but art had it under control all along, thank you very much) it brought me to tears.

Murray's acute self-consciousness is paralyzing, but also curiously freeing: It frees him up to be a rebel (just barely). In *The Razor's Edge*, he's the only character who is both (just) sane and (beautifully) whimsical, which is the balance he strikes in nearly every movie, his signature mixture of hip and square. He knows better than anyone else that you don't always have to do what they tell you to do, but he also tends to realize that the way out of the slough of despond is delight in other people, making him clubbable. In *Stripes,* asked by the drill sergeant what he's doing, Murray's character says, "Marching in a straight line, sir." It's not a straight line, but what he's doing is still, finally, marching. Although Murray is utterly insubordinate toward the sergeant, he winds up earning the sergeant's admiration by leading a rescue mission at the end. Murray is a goof-off and anti-establishment, but he winds up having the right stuff. He gets it together, but on his own terms, if "own terms" can be defined unambitiously. Asked by an interviewer what he thought of the television show *Cheers,* Murray said, "That was like prime-time TV; I never really got it or anything." Such is the extent of Murray's rebellion—late-night vs. prime-time TV. One of the many good jokes of *Tootsie* is that Murray, playing an avant-garde playwright, is nobody's idea of an avant-garde playwright: everything in his body—his competence, his responsibility—screams acceptance of things as they are. He defies without sabotaging authority. When an interviewer asked Murray whether *Rushmore* director Wes Anderson's gentle approach toward actors was effective, Murray replied, a bit huffily, "Well, that's good manners, you know? That's tact." Murray went to Loyola Academy, a prep school in Wilmette, and all his hell-raising is in a way the unthreateningly bad behavior of a slumming preppy. The ultimate effect of all his hijinks on the links is to deepen golf's hushed, moneyed silence

(Murray's antics would seem redundant at a football game). There's the official way and then there's your own way; Murray does it his own way, he never gets co-opted, but—and this is his magic trick, this is the movies, this is what is so deeply reassuring about his persona—he still succeeds (rids the city of ghosts, gets the girl, leads the rescue mission). He therefore is a perfect bridge figure between, to paint in broad strokes, Fifties conformity, Sixties rage, Seventies zaniness, Eighties and Nineties capitalismo; hence his appeal—he convinces us that we're still a little rebellious inside even as we're finally doing what everyone else is doing. As the child of left-wing activists, I'm frequently embarrassed by how bourgeois my yearnings are; Murray's relatively unangry versions of *épater le bourgeois* coat my conformity in glee.

This very deep contradiction in Murray is directly related to the way corrosive irony, in him, sits atop deep sentimentality. (So, too, for myself: Walking out of the theatre after *Terms of Endearment,* I subjected it to a withering critique while tears were still streaking down my face.) When he was guest commentator at a Chicago Cubs baseball game, he mocked every player on the opposing team in a parody of fan fanaticism ("That guy shouldn't even be in the major leagues, and he knows it. He's lying to himself; he really should go back into some sort of community service in his hometown"), but he refused every opportunity the cameraman handed him to score easy points off the enormously fat African-American umpire Eric Gregg, whose uniform had been lost and who just couldn't get comfortable in his borrowed clothes. Before the Cubs played their first night game at Wrigley Field, Murray visited the booth again, this time for just a few minutes, mercilessly ribbing the legendary announcer Harry Caray before suddenly declaring, "This is the most beautiful park in the world." I feel so earthbound compared to Murray, so uncelebratory. In *Ghostbusters,* he pretends to be a self-absorbed asshole, but we're meant to understand that underneath the mordant pose he's a pussycat. Murray's M.O. is in a way classic American cowboy—Gary Cooper, John Wayne, heart of gold, encased in steel. I'm the opposite—sensitivo surface masking homicidal maniac. Had the actors in *Mad Dog and Glory* been cast according to type—DeNiro playing the mobster and Murray the neurasthenic police photographer—the movie would have made no sense. The movie wouldn't be funny, the violence wouldn't seem silly, if we didn't understand that approximately credible though Murray is as the Mafia don, he's really not a killer, he's just joking, we don't believe him for a minute. Murray has an amazing ability to deliver mean lines that somehow don't sound mean; this is because he is, I'm almost sure of this, a gentle man (who also possesses of course perfectly repressed rage—giving the gentleness its edge). With just a few exceptions (*Kingpin,* say, or *Mad Dog and Glory*), Murray is almost always the character in the movie who embodies and articulates the vision of the movie, precisely because he's so hard to dislike. Asked about his parodies of bad singers, Murray explained, "You have to see what the original center of the song was and how they destroyed it. It's the ruining of a good song that you want to recreate. You have to like the stuff and you have to, I guess, know that when you have the microphone you have the opportunity to touch somebody. And when you don't do it with the lyric of it, and your own excuse for technique comes in and steps on top of it, that's, I guess, what I object to when I'm mimicking something." That old story: Rage is disappointed romanticism.

Disappointed romanticism, however, isn't romanticism. Murray isn't Tom Hanks; he never, or almost never, does romantic comedy. He likes himself too much, for as Murray says, "The romantic figure has to behave romantically even after acting like a total swine. It's, 'I'm so gorgeous you're going to have to go through all kinds of hell for me,' and that isn't interesting to me. Romance is very particular. There's something about romance, that if you don't have to have someone, you're more desirable." Murray has the dignity of not having to have someone, or at least not going on and on about it.

He is, in short, male, a guy's guy, still extremely boyish though he was born in 1950, broad-shouldered (6'1"), upbeat about his masculinity in a way that seems quite foreign and enviable to me. My voice is high and soft, as a way to control my stutter, but also as if in apology for my Y-chromosome. His father, who died when Murray was nineteen, was a lumber salesman. One of five brothers (and nine siblings), Murray now has five sons (and no daughters) from two marriages. So much of his persona, his shtick, his appeal is that he revels in and excels at the brutal but obviously affectionate teasing that is characteristic of large families, whereas more than one person has asked me, apropos of nothing in particular, whether I'm an only child (I'm not).

Occasionally psychotic but never neurotic, Murray plays well against nervous types, as I'm trying to make him do in this essay. He's not me. He's not Woody Allen. He's not Dustin Hoffman. In *Tootsie,* in which Dustin Hoffman plays an obnoxious actor, Michael Dorsey, who pretends to be a woman in order to get a part in a soap and, by "becoming" a woman, learns to be a better man, Murray is true north of "normal" masculinity, our ordinary-guy guide, the big galoot around whom the gender-bending bends. "I think we're getting into a weird area," he informs Hoffman when Hoffman gets preoccupied with his female alter ego's wardrobe. "Do you know what my problem is?" Hoffman asks him at one point. "Cramps?" Murray replies. When Hoffman asks Murray how he-as-she looks, Murray says, "Nice, but don't play hard to get." "Instead of trying to be Michael Dorsey the great actor or Michael Dorsey the great waiter," he advises Hoffman before ushering him in to his surprise birthday party, "why don't you just try to be Michael Dorsey?" This line isn't in even fairly late drafts of the screenplay; it's pure Murray; I'd bet he came up with it. He is the king of hanging out. He already knows how to be himself and how to be kind, how to be male but not be a jerk, whereas Hoffman needs to learn how to do this. Hoffman, the high-strung Jew, must learn how to do what Murray already does instinctively—to like life, to like the opposite sex, to embrace his own anima. *Live, live, live,* as Strether, that priss, finally realizes in Henry James's *The Ambassadors,* and as Murray has always known, as Murray always conveys.

Murray's boyishness is, at its most beguiling, childlikeness: openness to surprise. In *Cinderella Story: My Life in Golf,* Murray writes, "The sum and substance of what I was hoping to express is this. In golf, just as in life—I hoped I could get that line in the book somewhere [Murray's relentless ironic gaze, his ear for cliché]—the best wagers are laid on oneself." In *The Man Who Knew Too Little,* Murray plays Wallace Ritchie, a dim American

man who, visiting his businessman-brother in London, thinks
he's attending an avant-garde "Theatre of Life" performance and
unbeknownst to him is caught up in an international spy-versus-
spy scheme. Murray, as Ritchie, wins the day—defeats the bad
guys, gets the girl—because he just goes with the flow, is cool
and relaxed, never stops believing that he's watching and partici-
pating in an unusually realistic performance. Ritchie's relaxedness is Murray's relaxedness, Ritchie's distance is Murray's: Life
is theatre with arbitrary rules. His bemused bafflement toward
everything that happens is a handbook for Murray's acting technique and his approach to life—the absurdity of all action, but
(and therefore) grooving in the moment.

When Murray was the guest commentator at the Cubs game,
he somehow made anything the camera focused on—a hot dog
wrapper, an untucked shirt—seem newly resonant, of possible
interest, because unlike every person to ever broadcast a baseball
game, Murray talked about what was actually going on in his
head, was actually seeing what was going on in front of his eyes
rather than viewing it through a formulaic filter, was taking in
the entire ballpark rather than just the sporting event per se.
His eyes haven't gone dead yet. Life, seen through such eyes,
becomes existentially vivid. Broadcasting this game, Murray
seemed as interested in the physical universe as a beagle, sniff-
ing the ballpark for new sensory input. He's demonstrating the
Wildean wisdom that the only solution to the soul is the senses.
He's a combination of two characters from the movie *American
Beauty*: the kid with the video camera who can see ribbons of
beauty in a plastic bag being blown around in the wind, and the
Kevin Spacey character, who processes everything through his

sulphur-spewing irony machine. I'm Spacey and want to be the kid with the video camera.

It's Murray's attempt to be authentic, and underlining of his attempt to be authentic, that I admire most; all of my current aesthetic excitements derive from my boredom with the conventions of fiction and my hope that nonfiction (autobiography, confession, memoir, embarrassment, *something*) can perhaps produce something that is for me "truer," more "real." Lorne Michaels, the longtime producer of *Saturday Night Live*, once said, "It's a cliché, but Bill is always Bill. So much of my generation's approach to comedy was a reaction against the neediness of performers. When Bill was on stage, he didn't much care whether they [the audience] liked him. Because of that, he had enormous integrity. There was a way he always told the truth." The tape I have of Murray broadcasting the Cubs game has live audio rather than commercial breaks between innings; Murray sounds exactly the same off air as he does on. He is incapable of doing Stentorian Announcer let alone Star Turn. I adore this about him. At one point in his life he was strongly influenced by the philosophy of Gurdjieff, whose Madame Blavatskyesque work I can't bring myself to read but one of whose titles is *Life Is Only Real, Then, When "I Am."* A bad translation, to be sure, but the self-conscious quote marks around "I Am," the slight or not so slight inscrutability, the deep yearning to apprehend and embody reality—that's Murray's program.

The royal road to the authentic for Murray is through the primitive. Look at the Stanley Kowalski way he kicks open the door to the barracks in *Stripes*. In his self-interview, he told a joke about how Ralph Lauren's dog is named Rugby, but his real

name is Stickball. People who pretend that they are truly civi-
lized Murray finds ridiculous. In *Caddyshack,* a movie about class
warfare phrased as a golf comedy, he plays a groundskeeper who is
obsessed with killing gophers. Chevy Chase is the embodiment
of the golfing fop—moneyed, charming, handsome. Murray
is riddled by doubt, self-pitying, working-class ("I got a blue-
collar chip on my shoulder," Murray said. "That part of it was
not hard."). Chase, for all his bonhomie, isn't in touch with
the primitive force of the universe; Murray is (he's the only one
capable of recognizing that a dark brown clump floating in the
country club swimming pool isn't a turd but a Baby Ruth bar,
which he eats). The movie teaches the young golfer-protagonist
that Chase is wrong, Murray is right. The only way for Young
Golfer to grow up is by learning how to say fuck you to the
"snobatorium"—the country club's version of golf and life.

Would that rebellion were so easy. Still, when the interviewer
Charlie Rose advised Bill Murray to take a sabbatical, because
lawyers do, Murray said, "If law firms do it, Charlie, it probably can't be right." (That "probably" is quintessential Murray—
antiestablishmentarian but not utterly.) Rose also advised him
about the importance of "proportionality" in one's life—balance
between work and play. "I want to learn that one, too," Murray
said, pretending to search for a pencil. "Let me write it down."
In *Wild Things,* Murray is the lone actor among several other
middle-aged actors in the movie who is granted the privilege
of grasping the movie's vision: Human beings are beasts, life is
a scam, manipulate the other beasts in the jungle to your own
advantage. It would be impossible to cast Murray as someone
who didn't understand this.

Maybe it's not much of a revelation to anyone else, but to me it always seems to be: We're finally just physical creatures living in the physical world. Murray knows this in the bottom of his bones. If Murray didn't ad-lib the following lines in *Tootsie,* he should have: "I don't want a full house at the Winter Garden Theatre. I want ninety people who just came out of the worst rainstorm in the city's history. These are people who are alive on the planet, until they dry off. I wish I had a theatre that was only open when it rained." Explaining to an interviewer that *Rushmore* director Wes Anderson isn't just knowledgeable about film and clever about alluding to film history but also able to convey strong emotion in his work, Murray said, "Let's get right down to it. It's like the French. You know, they can't play rock-'n'-roll to save their lives. They can't play the blues to save their lives. But if you play a song by somebody, you know, Son House, they go, 'That's Son House, the famous musician and blues player. That is from the session he did in Meridian, Mississippi. I believe that is the January 24th . . . ' You know, they'll know the date, the time, and the take. They couldn't give you an ounce of the feeling of it, you know. But this guy, Wes, and it's the difference, you know—mind and body, he just knows how to get these things together in one place." Murray does the same thing; all his verbal play happens atop a foundation of understated physical grace. In *Space Jam,* Murray isn't Michael Jordan, but it's crucial that he isn't Wayne Knight, either. He's halfway between jock god and blubbery nerd—someone we can identify with. After kibitzing with Michael Jordan at the golfing tee, wearing madras shorts and cornball shirt and shoes, he finally whacks the hell out of the ball. So, too, at pro-am tournaments it wouldn't work if, after goofing around for twenty minutes, he couldn't finally play the game. By being both ridiculous and competent, he becomes beautifully contradictory—the unicycle-riding knife juggler who pretends to be anxiety-stricken but isn't; without the contradiction he's just pathetic (Wayne Knight) or boringly excellent (Jordan). It's that stage in between that Murray occupies so movingly.

I imagine that Murray would be a bit of a bully in the way a hip older brother or popular camp counselor might be—making you feel bad if you just don't want to have fun right now as Murray defines fun, not allowing you to just mope if that's what you want to do. I imagine he would be such a drill sergeant on this score—toward his sons, say—because a frenetically kept-up *joie de vivre* is how he's managed to paper over his fairly real despair, and if he can, he's going to bring everyone along with him out of hell. I admire this and resent it a little; why can't we mope if we want to mope? Maybe the only solution to the soul isn't the senses; maybe it's deeper soul-searching (probably not); maybe there is no soul. "To be, to be, sure beats the shit out of not to be," he writes at the end of *The Cinderella Story.* At the very end of *Where the Buffalo Roam,* in which Murray plays Hunter Thompson, Murray quotes Lord Buckley's epitaph: "He stomped on the terra." This is the nucleus of Murray: We're made of clay; we better cause a little ruckus while we can. He's the anti-Malvolio in our midst; he's Tigger versus the suits. Life is absurd—make it your own absurdity. Instead of wearing artiste basic-black—my dumb uniform—Murray typically wears his own weird mix of plaids and prints of different patterns and colors—a tartan vest, for instance, with a paisley tie, and a sky-blue shirt. Or black pants, a brown striped shirt, and a tan vest. Nutty clothes—so out they're in, cool because he's wearing them.

In *What About Bob?* Murray, as Bob Wylie, the patient of anhedonic psychiatrist Leo Marvin (the un-Lee Marvin), visits the Marvins' summer home and succeeds in making even dish-washing, for Chrissake, fun for Marvin's family, though not for Dr. Marvin, of course. Murray and Dreyfuss reportedly came to despise each other in the making of the movie—Murray's unscripted silliness drove Dreyfuss crazy, in exactly the same way Bob drives Leo mad in the movie—and I know we're supposed to love Murray and hate Dreyfuss, and I do, I do, but I'm much closer to serious, striving Dr. Marvin than I am to antic Bob, which is, I suppose, what this essay is about: my distance from Murray, my yearning to be him, the gap between us, the way he makes life seem bearable (fun, amusing) if I could only get with his giddiness. (I can't.) In Murray's golf book, Cheryl Anderson, a golf pro, says, "I was practicing at the far end of the grand cypress range one morning. There wasn't another soul there. Just a set of clubs in one of the stands a few yards away from me. Then a figure appeared in the distance. He was on a bicycle, at the same time carrying a boom box. It was Bill. He gave me a quick nod, then walked to the clubs, set down his box, and flipped on a tape. It was an out-there rock group called Big Head Todd and the Monsters. He hit balls to the music for a while, then picked up the box, nodded goodbye, and pedaled off."

Physical grace as a container, then, for spiritual grace, if that's not putting too fine a point on it. "A lot of *Rushmore* is about the struggle to retain civility and kindness in the face of extraordinary pain," Murray said shortly after the film was released. "And I've felt a lot of that in my life." This is what Murray knows so well and what I have been trying to learn from him: Life is a shit-storm; laugh (somehow and barely). In his self-interview, he tells Santa a story about the making of the movie *Scrooged*: "We're shooting in this Victorian set for weeks, and [Buddy] Hackett is pissed all the time, angry that he's not the center of attention, and finally we get to the scene where we've gotta shoot him at the window, saying, 'Go get my boots,' or whatever. The set is stocked with Victorian extras and little children in Oliver kind of outfits, and the director says, 'All right, Bud, just give it whatever you want.' And Hackett goes off on a rant. Unbelievably obscene. He's talking—this is Hackett, not me—about the Virgin Mary, a limerick sort of thing, and all these children and families . . . the look of absolute horror. He's going on and on and on, and finally he stops. It's just total horror, and the camera's still rolling. You can hear it, sort of a grinding noise. And the director says, 'Anything else, Bud?'" Murray loves the director's dignity against the shit-storm, his refusal to be cowed or fazed.

In his article "The Passion of Bill Murray," Greg Solman writes about Murray's performance in *Mad Dog and Glory*, "What's remarkable about the performance is how well Murray can now convey the intrinsic humor of his characters and situations . . . but differentiate them from others in his past by eliminating irony, sarcasm, and self-reflexivity." This seems to me wrong, or at least in opposition to the premise of this essay: namely, that in the twenty-five years Murray has been acting he's gotten better not by ever going away for a second from irony but by finding deeper and deeper levels of emotion

within it. That's why I value his work so much: He embodies
the way—not around but through. At the end of *Groundhog
Day*, after being forced to repeat February 2nd over and over
again until he discovers real feeling, he finally says to a sleeping
Andie McDowell, "I think you're the kindest, sweetest, prettiest
person I've ever met in my life. I've never seen anyone that's
nicer to people than you are. The first time I saw you, something happened to me that I never told you about. I knew
that I wanted to hold you as hard as I could. I don't deserve
someone like you, but if I ever could, I swear I would love you
for the rest of our life." This is awfully sweet, and the only rea-
son I believe it is because of the way Murray teases her when
he's teaching her how to flip cards into a hat. At the end of
Scrooged, Murray, the scabrous president of a television net-
work who recovers the Christmas spirit, walks onto the set of
the cheesy, live Christmas special he's produced, announcing:
"It's Christmas Eve. It's the one night of the year where we all
act a little nicer, we smile a little easier, we cheer a little more.
For a couple of hours out of the whole year we are the people
that we always hoped we would be. It's a miracle, it's really
a sort of a miracle, because it happens every Christmas Eve.
You'll want it every day of your life, and it can happen to you.
I believe in it now. I believe it's going to happen to me now.
I'm ready for it." A few moments later, when he has trouble
dragging his long lost beloved, Claire, in front of the camera,
Murray, clearly improvising, says, "This is like boning a mar-
lin." It's Murray's fidelity to his own mordant consciousness
and the locating of joy within that mordancy that is, to me, the
miracle. This is getting a little overadulatory, so I'll stop.

An unfortunate fact about stuttering is that it prevents you from ever entirely losing self-consciousness when expressing such traditional and truly important emotions as love, hate, joy, and deep pain. Always first aware not of the naked feeling itself but of the best way to phrase the feeling so as to avoid verbal repetition, you come to think of emotions as belonging to other people, being the world's happy property and not yours—not really yours except by way of disingenuous circumlocution. Hence my iron grip on ironic distance; hence my adoration of Murray; hence my lifelong love of novels (*The Great Gatsby*, *A Separate Peace*, Ford Madox Ford's *The Good Soldier*, Gunter Grass's *Cat and Mouse*) in which a neurasthenic narrator contemplates his more vital second self; hence this essay. My first novel is about a sportswriter's vicarious relationship with a college basketball player; my most recent book, a diary of an NBA season, is largely given over to my obsession with Gary Payton. What is it about such a relationship that speaks so strongly to me? Art calling out to Life, unLife wanting Life? Are these just parts of myself in eternal debate or am I really this anemic? Murray, for all his anomie, likes being in the world. Bully for him. I love standing in shadow, gazing intently at ethereal glare.

Blindness

—◊◊—

BOBBY KNIGHT, *C'EST MOI.*

No, I've never hit a Puerto Rican policeman before practice at the Pan American Games, stuffed a fan from an opposing team in a garbage can, told Connie Chung, "I think that if rape is inevitable, relax and enjoy it," told women, "There's only two things you people are good for: having babies and frying bacon," pretended to bull-whip my star player, waved used toilet paper in my players' faces to provide them with a metaphor for their poor play, tossed a chair across the court during a game, kicked my son—a player on the team—in the leg during another game, head-butted another player during another game, or choked another player during practice. But neither have I won three

NCAA championships, twice been named Coach of the Year, coached the United States to an Olympic gold medal, won over 700 college basketball games, or had a higher graduation rate among my players than nearly any other Division I basketball coach.

Me? Because I stutter, I became a writer (in order to return to the scene of the crime and convert the bloody fingerprints into Abstract Expressionism). As a writer, I love language as much as any element in the universe, but I also have trouble living anywhere other than in language. If I'm not writing it down, experience doesn't really register. Language has gone from prison to refuge back to prison. Bobby Knight once said, "All of us learn to write by the second grade, then most of us go on to other things."

Is it clear yet how Knight and I are alike? In short, what animates us inevitably ails us. Not only for Knight and me, of course, but for everybody. What was largely absent from all the coverage and commentary following Knight's dismissal from Indiana University for violating its "zero-tolerance" policy is recognition on anyone's part that for all of us, the force for good can convert so frighteningly easily into force for ill, that our deepest strength is indivisible from our most embarrassing weakness, that what makes us great will inexorably get us in terrible trouble. Everyone's ambition is underwritten by a tragic flaw.

"A great painting comes together," Picasso said, "just barely." That fine edge gets harder and harder to maintain. As I indicated earlier, I yield to no one in my admiration of Renata Adler's first novel, *Speedboat;* it is, I think, one of the most original and formally exciting American novels published in the last twenty-five years. And I hesitate to heap any more dispraise upon her recent much-maligned memoir, *Gone,* which I must admit I found utterly addictive. But surely the difference between *Speedboat* and *Gone* has to do with the fact that in the earlier book the panic-tone is beautifully modulated and under complete control, even occasionally mocked, whereas in the later book it's been given, somewhat alarmingly, absolutely free reign. Success breeds self-indulgence. What was effectively bittersweet turns toxic.

We all contrive different, wonderfully idiosyncratic and revealing ways to remain blind to our own blindnesses. In the British television series *Cracker,* Eddie Fitzgerald is a brilliant forensic psychologist who can solve the riddle of every dark human heart except of course his own (he gambles nonstop, drinks nonstop, smokes nonstop, is fat, and estranged from his wife). Richard Nixon had to undo himself, because—as hard as he worked to get there—he didn't believe he belonged there. Bill Clinton's fatal charm is his charming fatality: His magnetism is his doom; they're the same trait. Someone recently said to me about Clinton, "By all accounts he could have been, should have been, one of the great presidents of the twentieth-century, so it's such a shame that . . ." No. No. No. There's no "if only" in human nature; it's all one brutal feedback loop.

And when our difficult heroes self-destruct—within a week of being hired by Texas Tech, Knight threw three players off the team for an unspecified "violation of team rules"—watch us retreat and reassure ourselves that it's safer here close to shore, where we live. We want the good in them, the gift in them, not the nastiness, or so we pretend. Publicly, we *tsk-tsk,* chastising their transgressions.

Secretly, we thrill to their violations, their (psychic or physical) violence, because through them we vicariously renew our acquaintance with our own shadow side. By detaching, though, before free-fall, we preserve our distance from death, stave off at any cost serious knowledge about the exact mixture in ourselves of the angel and the animal.

In college, when I read Greek tragedies and commentaries upon them, I would think, rather blithely, "Well, that tragic flaw thing is nicely symmetrical: Whatever makes Oedipus heroic is also—" What did I know then? Nothing. I didn't feel in my bones as I do now that what powers our drive assures our downfall, that our birthdate is our death sentence. You're fated to kill your dad and marry your mom, so they send you away. You live with your new mom and dad, find out about the curse, run off and kill your real dad, marry your real mom. It was a set-up. You had to test it. Even though you knew it would cost you your eyes, you had to do it. You had to push ahead. You had to prove who you are.

Acknowledgments

—ᴍ—

THANKS TO Steve Cramer, Stephanie Gunn, and Jan Wojcik for their contributions to "On Views and Viewing," and to Samantha Ruckman for her collaboration with me on "Possible Postcards from Rachel, Abroad." My deep gratitude to Peter Bailey, whose generous and rigorous response to my work is central to my writing life and this book in particular.